SENSUOUS SPACES

Designing Your Erotic Interiors

SENSUOUS SPACES

by Sivon Reznikoff

WHITNEY LIBRARY OF DESIGN
an imprint of Watson-Guptill Publications/New York

First published 1983 in New York by Whitney Library of Design,
an imprint of Watson-Guptill Publications,
a division of Billboard Publications, Inc.,
1515 Broadway, New York, N.Y. 10036

Library of Congress Cataloging in Publication Data
Reznikoff, S. C.
   Sensuous spaces.
   Bibliography: p.
   Includes index.
   1. Interior decoration—Psychological aspects.
2. Erotica.   I. Title.
NK2113.R49   1983   747   83-12490
ISBN 0-8230-7176-6

Distributed in the United Kingdom by Phaidon Press Ltd., Littlegate
House, St. Ebbe's St., Oxford

Manufactured in Japan

1 2 3 4 5 6 7 8 9/88 87 86 85 84 83

DISCLAIMER
The information and statements herein are believed to be
reliable but are not to be construed as a warranty or
representation for which the author or publishers assume
legal responsibility. Users should undertake sufficient
verification and testing to determine the suitability for their
own particular purpose of any information or products
referred to herein. **No warranty of fitness for a
particular purpose is made.**
   Nothing herein is to be taken as permission, induce-
ment, or recommendation to practice any patented
invention without a license. The author bears no legal
responsibility for any misrepresentation or contradiction
of contents projected by the published title.

Photographs of Paul Rudolph's work on pages 128,
173–175: Courtesy HOUSE & GARDEN. Copyright ©
1976, 1977 by the Condé Nast Publications Inc.

Edited by Stephen A. Kliment and Susan Davis
Designed by Jay Anning
Graphic production by Hector Campbell
Set in 11 point Bodoni Roman

For Tamara Adena, my romantic, seductive, and sensuous daughter

Contents

Foreword

The idea that objects, parts of the body, people, and experience can be invested with sexual feeling has become widely accepted as a normal, healthy part of life. Eroticism was conceptualized by Freud, the first psychoanalytic thinker, as beginning in infancy (without the implications of adult sexuality). He concluded that the process of maturing involves redirecting this from oneself to the external world. Recent ultrasound studies of fetuses in the womb show that males regularly have erections, indicating that sexuality in children starts even before birth. Many theories of mental illness blame distortions and maladaptations of the infant and child's manner of dealing with sexual and other drives as one causative factor. Fantasies and dreams are seen as safe outlets for drives that might otherwise be prohibited. These fantasies and dreams may not even have a sexual theme.

Carl Jung focused on the concept of the universality and collective nature of some symbols. Examples of erotic symbolism abound in comparative studies of different cultures, religions, and mythologies. Although considered radical in his time, these ideas are currently accepted today.

Contemporary erotic symbolism is normally experienced and expressed in many socially accepted forms. Dancing is one example. Advertising is the most obvious application of the universality of erotic symbolism in that it relies on the use of symbolism to exploit the "erotization" of products. This is readily seen in the merchandising of such personal products as perfumes and clothing.

Certain expressions of eroticism are considered "feminine" or "masculine" in our society. This division is seen in activities that are denoted as being masculine or feminine, such as types of work and sports, as well as in what we wear, although with the recent focus on equality for women some of these distinctions have become blurred. For example, women have adopted many "masculine" forms of dress such as different types of trousers, and men have begun to display some items of jewelry previously considered "feminine," such as neck chains and even pierced earrings. Although these examples of eroticism have become less gender-specific, others remain distinct, with some stylized clothes considered high fashion and quite erotic. Differences in fantasies and other more explicit expressions of eroticism remain.

Relationships are also eroticized, and they are influenced by events of our times as well as popular customs. Changes have caused various societal repercussions, some of which include increases in alcohol and drug abuse, disruptions of the extended family, feelings of social alienation, as well as changes in erotic relationships. The influences on expressions and experiences of eroticism have been manifested in many forms. One example is the so-called Sexual Revolution with its initial focus on casual relationships and the physical aspects of sexual activity. During the past decade pressures have also had a dichotomous effect on erotic relationships: While the rate of divorce has been increasing, there has been a converse desire by many to achieve greater degrees of intimacy. This is seen in the increasing demand for couple and family therapy, the popularity of the marriage encounter movement, and the burgeoning of various psychotherapies and encounter groups to help achieve self-awareness and greater ease with intimacy. These changes in relationships have also been mirrored in the design of our internal spaces, both public and private. Notable in this respect have been the advent of the disco, which almost prohibits intimacy, and the bachelor pad, which connotes shallow erotic relationships.

A great deal of scholarly and popular attention has been directed to the mysterious expressions of eroticism in dreams and fantasies. Much effort has also been given to the study of overt manifestations of eroticism in our dress, possessions, and activities. There has been a paucity of information, however, about eroticism associated with interior spaces. This book is unique and important, therefore, because it represents a systematic study of how we eroticize our interior spaces, focusing primarily on the most personal rooms of our environment, especially the bedroom. These spaces, which we design, color, and furnish, are important because they reflect eroticism and also serve to stimulate erotic dreams, fantasies, and relationships. The distinctions between masculine and feminine are also revealed in the uses of and reactions to interior spaces.

Professor Sivon Reznikoff has been able to integrate the concepts of how events and attitudes of various epochs affect the erotization of interior spaces and their effects on relationships. She demonstrates how relationships are influenced by the design of environments and how they also reflect our perceived need to establish different types of relationships.

I was pleased to advise and assist Professor Reznikoff in bringing out this vanguard publication. Her observations, insights, and conceptualizations offer a unique elaboration of another aspect of human behavior.

This book should be of interest to a wide audience, including designers, architects, students of human behavior, and those who may want to learn more about themselves and make their spaces and their lives more enjoyable.

Darryl R. Stern, M.D.
Diplomate, American Board
of Psychiatry and Neurology

Acknowledgments

This book would not have been possible without the assistance of the designers and photographers who generously shared their knowledge of romantic, seductive, and sensuous spaces. This book was further enriched by many artisans and manufacturers who provided examples of art, as well as custom-designed and mass-produced objects that can fulfill our most demanding fantasies and enhance our intimate environments.

Annette Green, the dynamic director of the Fragrance Foundation in New York City, generated information that verified my theories concerning relationships between spatial sensory engineering and the science of fragrance engineering. The conceptual diagrams developed by Naarden International further clarified that two seemingly unrelated fields are both concerned with understanding and meeting deep human needs.

Special thanks to Carol S. King, Editor of *Designers West*, who introduced me to many talented West Coast designers. I appreciated the assistance of Joy Tormey, whose ability to grasp conceptual meanings made her a valuable member of the research team. The able assistance of Vito Dascoli and John McKelvey also contributed to the success of this project.

In the early research phases Polly and John Hendel's life story provided insights into the timeless universal quality of romantic love. Others that provided support, inspiration, opinions, and critical evaluations far exceed this space, but among the most notable are Marge and Harry Payne, Marcelle Resnikoff Opper, Ann Patterson, Barbara Powell, Sharon Stevens, Philip Mazzurco, Fran Nolan, and Betty J. Wagner. I am deeply grateful for the support and understanding of my colleagues Marcus Whiffin, Gerald R. McSheffrey, Tom Witt, Mary Shipley, Mike Kroelinger, Mike Nielsen and my life-long mentor, Professor Gulnar K. Bosch, who assisted in proofreading during the final hours.

Senior Editor Stephen A. Kliment, FAIA, diligently located obscure photographic sources and communicated with people who normally only commune with the Gods. His keen intellectual insight and insistence on research evidence was responsible for the numerous tree and bar diagrams that add dimension to the concepts in this book.

The author will be forever indebted to the emotional insights and the determined psychic energies of Development Editor Susan Davis who traveled thousands of miles to preserve the essence of this book. For her efforts, she subsequently received the "Erotic Soft Disk Award."

The entire Whitney Library "family," including Executive Editor David Lewis, the long-suffering Art Department, the promotional staff, and the sales representatives from Europe and the North American continent deserve recognition for producing a successful book and proving that sublimation is still a viable force in contemporary life.

Special appreciation is extended to psychiatrist Darryl Stern, M.D., who served as research consultant to the author throughout the development and editing of the manuscript.

Introduction

You may have purchased this book for a number of reasons:

1. Your "sexy" bedroom, complete with mirrored ceilings and walls, does not seem quite as impressive as it once did.

2. You have settled into the routine of a marriage or a lengthy affair that is bordering on rigor mortis.

3. You are just getting your first apartment, condominium, or home and can finally give some serious thought to creating spaces that are really yours.

4. You have just emerged from a long marriage with no idea of how to start over, much less who you are.

5. You have a client who wants the sexiest bedroom west of the Atlantic.

Whatever your reasons, you want to know more about erotic interiors and how they can add a new dimension to your life.

Bear in mind that your interest in adding excitement to your life is shared by many. Glance over any weekly list of best-selling books, or notice what your fellow commuters are reading on the bus, plane, or train. Subjects range from romantic adventures to step-by-step instructional manuals on how to lose weight and regain youthful, sexual attractiveness. This innate human yearning for self-improvement, variety, and excitement is part of the universal life instinct.

A great many of our attitudes, and some of the most dynamic erotic spaces, are the result of the Sexual Revolution of the sixties. While that revolution encouraged people to become more open and direct about basic sexual needs, it also triggered personal conflicts that are reflected in many aspects of our lives. For example, the books we are reading illustrate that we have become accustomed to seeking solutions from anyone who will give crystal-ball predictions and promise the "how-to's" of getting our lives in order.

This book does not provide another decorating "quick fix," but it will help you gain control of your multidimensional sense of awareness. Many of us have become inadvertently locked into a self-imposed level of awareness that stifles creative thinking. The interior spaces in this book, however, have been evaluated on three distinct levels of awareness.

1. Name-Tag Level of Awareness. This level of awareness provides a sense of physical and intellectual security. When we are unable to categorize or identify an object it immediately becomes suspect. When earth-shaking cultural changes become stressful we turn to our own self-styled label-inventing experts and gurus (also known as "movers and shakers") who use their oracular visions to identify "trends." (When something has been around long enough to merit a label it is no longer a trend but has become a *fashion* or *style*.) In 1980 *The New York Times* architectural critic Ada Louise Huxtable noted that "intellectual trendiness" had become rampant.* Her fears were confirmed in the summer of 1983 when a designers' conference listed a seminar to explain the following new "trends": New Design, New Wave, New International Style, Memphis, Ocean Liner Aesthetic, New Ornamentalism, Post High-Tech, Post Industrial, Hypermodern, Post Sub-Modern, and Post Modernism.

In order to avoid causing anyone distress, the spaces in this book will be carefully labeled with such titles as "romantic, seductive, and sensuous." But remember that name-tagging, trend-watching, and guru-ism can become so time-consuming you may

*Ada Louise Huxtable, "The Troubled State of Architecture," *Progressive Architecture*, 1981.

never want to move on to the next level of awareness.

2. The Intellectual Take-a-Closer-Look Level. This technical level of awareness allows people to notice small, but significant details, such as the direction of the brush stroke in a painting. Or while reading this page you may become aware of grammar, sentence structure, and punctuation. This book will point out small, but important details of erotic interiors, such as textures, colors, special lighting, and other aspects only noticeable to the trained eye of the designer. This level can be very rewarding, but beware of myopic vision that could limit your full range of awareness.

3. The Insight Level of Awareness. The third and highest level of awareness releases creative imagination. It allows people to survey past, present, and future implications and arrive at the essence of meanings through emotional insights that preclude pragmatic categorizing. The psychological implications, the ancient symbolism, and the universal fantasy cues that make the erotic spaces in this book unique will enhance your enjoyment of space.

One rarely gets locked into this level because its very essence reveals the rhythmic nature of all things, thus allowing us to roam freely among all three levels of awareness.

The research for this book often involved identifying the subtle cultural aftershocks generated by events and attitudes implanted generations ago. Because the pragmatic may have a problem with psychological concepts that cannot be directly observed or measured in a mathematical manner, analogies have been used to help demystify certain theories. After you have overcome labels and stigmatized words, may your enjoyment of spaces be surpassed only by the happiness of fulfilled fantasies.

WHY EROTIC ENVIRONMENTS

1

What Are Erotic Spaces and Where Can You Find Them?

If you have always associated "erotic" with something sexy and perhaps even naughty, it may be difficult to start thinking about erotic spaces as very normal outward displays of a universal human need. This need was defined by Sigmund Freud when he introduced the theory of Eros as the life-giving force. To Freud all the life-giving instincts, not just sexuality, were included under the heading of "Eros." It is this innate psychic energy force, for instance, that drives you to get up in the morning, ask for that raise, and strive to realize your ambitions. In this context, then, erotic spaces are visible expressions of the universal life instinct.

Spaces become erotic, or eroticized, according to psychiatrists, when people charge them with varying degrees of erotic psychic energy. This energy can be compared with an electrical current that may range from a tiny spark to a high-voltage charge. These scientists are not referring to some advanced technique developed in a sex clinic, but to an innate power source that everyone possesses.

Cinderella's godmother transformed a pumpkin into a coach, but erotic energy transformed a garbage truck into a chapel of love for an Arizona couple. The groom who loved his work as an equipment mechanic at the sanitation department proposed that the marriage take place inside one of the trucks. After the ceremony their friends formed a wrench honor guard. Instead of rice, tiny packets of grease-absorbing granules were tossed by more than one hundred guests. (Arizona Republic)

Everyone has the ability to eroticize people, places, and things. Although people usually project this energy unconsciously,[1] we often refer to it when discussing personal relationships: "There was instant charisma between us." "He really turned me on." "The chemistry was right." Psychologists note that everytime we use the word "love" to describe something we enjoy—"I love this restaurant," for example—we have actually energized or eroticized that object or activity with psychic energy.[2] How many references to erotic energy can you think of in songs and advertisements?

To find erotic spaces just look around—they are everywhere: both in nature settings and in man-made spaces; at the seashore, in a cabin on a mountain top, in a restaurant, and certainly in your own home.

Our need to eroticize, however, may also show up in the most unpredictable and amazing places. For example, how many of your friends would understand why you want to drive a hundred miles to visit an old roadside diner that reeks of recycled bacon grease, only because it was where you met your first great love. Or consider the seemingly illogical psychic energy that can transform a garbage truck into a "chapel of love" for a couple's wedding.

[1]American Psychiatric Association, *A Psychiatric Glossary*, Washington, D.C., 1976, p. 53.

[2]Robert M. Goldberg, Ph.D., *The Encyclopedia of Human Behavior: Psychology, Psychiatry, and Mental Health*, vol. 1, Garden City, N.Y.: Doubleday and Company, 1970, p. 415.

Having eroticized a particular space, we will spare no expense to protect it from natural disasters such as floods and violent wind storms. In the early 1980s a couple living in the California redwood forest created a 1500-pound steel frame to protect their bed from the possibility of falling trees. The huge frame had a shiny sheet metal canopy for "limb protection," and the entire unit was bolted to the house foundation.

CAUTION: This book is not about good taste or about good design versus bad design. Rather than casting judgments, moral, aesthetic, or otherwise, this book presents a broad view of eroticism that will help you gain insights into some of your basic needs that may not be openly addressed by the interior spaces you presently occupy. Spaces that meet a human need should not be evaluated solely on the basis of taste or fashion. But if your need involves displaying "good taste," then make it one of your criterion.

Is there more than one type of erotic space?

Erotic spaces can be as varied as the needs and circumstances that produced them. When these spaces are viewed as the settings needed to *develop and sustain* certain types of human relationships, they take on important social significance. It's easy to identify such relationships in the business world. Everyone recognizes that the offices occupied by the corporate president and vice-presi-

The very foundation of society—and the purity of the family—rests on the obligation to protect the sanctity of the bedroom and its contents. A couple living in a redwood forest in California designed and built a 1500-pound steel frame to protect their bed against the danger of falling trees. Instead of a mirrored canopy, it is covered in metal to prevent smaller branches from crashing through. (World Wide Photos)

dents represent their place in the corporate power structure. In our private lives, however, we are often not aware of how spaces reflect our intimate relationships. These relationships evolve in a series of overlapping phases with each a *necessary prelude* to the next. For example, our erotic life can be divided into three phases:

1. The first could be called entry-level eroticism, or the *romantic* stage. In phase one we imbue each other with low-level psychic energy as we get acquainted.

2. Having verified that original interest and attraction, we move into phase two and begin to express a medium level of psychic energy in the *seductive* process.

3. In the third and final phase *sensuous* contact produces intense psychic energy levels, which seek immediate release.

Based on this concept of *evolving* intimate relationships, this book will examine interior spaces according to the following three categories: romantic, seductive, and sensuous.

If you are surprised to find romantic spaces included in a book about erotic interiors, you are expressing well-established Victorian attitudes. By sublimating what was obviously sexual into the romantic, Victorians succeeded in separating the romantic from the erotic. The romantic became the public face of Eros and allowed sexual instincts to be expressed in proper social channels, rather than remain dammed-up.[3]

During the Sexual Revolution, however, everything romantic was bypassed because people no longer considered it a channel necessary for erotic expression. But that too had its short-comings. Placing an almost exclusive emphasis on seductive encounters began to short circuit the natural sequence of many relationships. By the early eighties magazine and newspaper articles proclaimed that the Sexual Revolution was losing out to boredom.[4] Couples were finding it more and more difficult to regain that old "spark." Singles were finding it hard to know where to go next

[3]Kaplan, Freedman, and Sadock, *Comprehensive Textbook of Psychiatry*, vols. 1–3, Baltimore, Md.: Williams and Wilkins Company, 1980, chap. 8, p. 692.

[4]"Sexual Revolution Losing out to Boredom, Expert Says," *The Arizona Republic*, Oct. 3, 1980.

after the discos and the singles bars made it all so easy and instant. How could anyone be bored? But the message was unmistakably clear. Throughout the country women snapped up clothing with nostalgic lace and ruffles, and millions began reading romantic novels. Couples began searching for romantic weekend retreats, and after finding how exciting it was to hold hands by candlelight, many were also interested in learning how to dance cheek to cheek to the Big Band music popular in the forties. People began to sense the importance of investing time and energy in forming lasting relationships. The Sexual Revolution appeared to have come full circle.

Can erotic spaces help you form relationships?

Depending on the social climate, erotic spaces can provide settings that encourage or discourage the development of relationships. For instance, the Sexual Revolution encouraged us to take pride in maintaining a lack of attachment, to keep aloof and cool. Discos reflected this trend. They were not designed to encourage conversation or an investment of time. They were designed for dancing and cruising—making eye contact only during the split-second flash of a strobe light.

To test your attitudes about space, take the following quiz.

1. What interior space would you visit to pick up a quick date?

2. What setting would you select for a wedding anniversary dinner?

Your answers to these questions illustrate that you have different *preconceived expectations* about spaces. Think how differently you respond to a place of worship versus a health club, or a fast-foods chain and a library. The quality of our relationships is definitely affected by the mental blueprints we have about spaces.

If an erotic space can help you form relationships, then, you may ask, can it also make you more exciting? The answer to that question depends on how you and the space interact. Perhaps what you are really asking is: "Can erotic spaces actually transform the toad into the prince?"

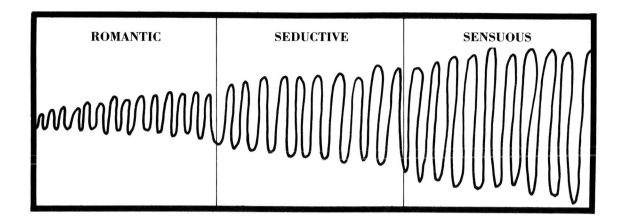

| ROMANTIC | SEDUCTIVE | SENSUOUS |

The bachelor pads that appeared in the sixties promised all this and more. They were among the most highly publicized and photographed spaces in the last three decades. They became a prized status symbol for many unmarried men, second only to their sports cars. The mystique of the bachelor pad was that it somehow guaranteed the owner successful sexual conquests or gave the impression that many exciting encounters had taken place there. These erotic spaces began to malfunction when everyone began duplicating them without customizing the space to their own fantasies.

Yes, erotic interiors can make your life more exciting, but only if you supply the erotic energy.

Which erotic space is best for you?

You may have already decided you are the romantic type, or you may pride yourself on being too sophisticated for all that mushy stuff. If you think, however, that only one type of erotic space will meet your needs, then you have missed the point. *WARNING:* Trying to typecast yourself can be dangerous to your mental health. It can stunt your growth and the growth of the relationships in your life. The person who always dines at the same restaurant because "I don't like surprises" is probably the same person who wants sex only on Fridays after the late news. Like summer television viewing, our lives can become an unending series of reruns.

But, you may be thinking, don't men and women need *different* types of erotic spaces.

That all depends on the type and level of erotic energy needed by the individual, but research has shown that the modus operandi of the female makes her less likely to bypass the entry-level phase of eroticism. Because romantic spaces represent love, family, permanence, and all the other things responsible for the formation of relationships, our culture has traditionally associated romantic spaces with women.[5]

Throughout this book you will see private erotic spaces occupied by males and females, living alone or with a partner. These spaces offer fresh insights into the subtle differences between male and female spaces—although such differences do vary depending on the individual.

Are erotic interiors a passing fad?

Erotic interiors have been around a long time; they will be a part of our environment as long as people interact. If you are afraid that someone will think you outrageous because of your unique use of space, this book will show you that someone else probably thought of the same solution hundreds of years ago.

Whether old or new, the spaces you will see in the following chapters illustrate the many means of realizing your romantic, seductive, and sensuous dreams. The next chapter will explore the many components that you can use to design your own erotic spaces.

[5]Carol Gilligan, "Why Should a Woman Be More Like a Man?," *Psychology Today*, June 1982, pp. 68–74.

This diagram shows the growth of psychic energy needed to sustain evolving intimate relationships. In entry-level romanticism the energy level is low, but increases rapidly as it moves through the seductive phase and finally reaches the sensuous phase where it finds release. The erotic wheel shown on page 16 further explains the rhythmic flow of psychic energy.

The erotic wheel
illustrates the concept
of Eros as a life-giving
energy source that
activates the three
equally important
phases of intimate
relationships.

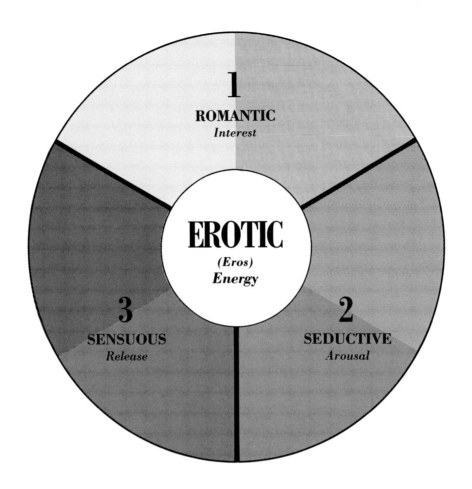

	Romantic	Seductive	Sensuous
Moods, feelings provoked	Passion Fascination Infatuation Appeal Affection Nostalgia Awe Tenderness Glamor Playfulness	Attraction Allure Enticement Charm Lure Dazzle Captivation Playfulness Temptation	Voluptuousness Opulence Abundance Intimacy Playfulness Spontaneity Instinct Intuition Luxury Ecstasy Yielding
Colors	Soft	Bright, intense, vivid	Deep, rich
Forms	Soft	Rounded	Undulating, curved
Textures	Soft: velvets	Soft: fur	Smooth: satins
Music	Waltz Piano concertos Violins	Tango	Bolero Hard rock El Amor Brujo
Fragrance	Flowers Citrus Modern floral blends	Woodsy Mossy Fruit Spice	Animal (boise) Floral blends Amber Spice
Temperature	Warm	Simmering	Boiling, hot
Places	Public: secluded restaurants Nature: lakes, mountain tops, sea or lake shore	Semipublic Bars, clubs Residential	Intimate Hotels, resorts Residential

2

The Sensory Engineering Approach

I f everyone is capable of eroticizing their own space what is sensory engineering? The term "sensory engineering" will be used in this book to describe the process of creating erotic spaces. Defining it, for instance, can be as difficult as trying to describe the person you love to someone else or as difficult as expressing your feelings to another person. You may want to write a love letter or a poem, but after hours of trying to compose the sentences, you may still feel awkward and inadequate. In desperation, you carefully search through rows of greeting cards until you find one that sums up your sentiments. To further show the intensity of your emotions you may resort to flowers, a gift of perfume, or a romantic dinner in a small cafe where you ask the orchestra to play "your" love song to get the message across. Without realizing it, you have used the services of several sensory engineers.

What is a sensory engineer?

A sensory engineer is the poet who wrote the greeting card that expressed your feelings. A sensory engineer is the composer of the music that captured your erotic energy level. Sensory engineers projected your feelings in that captivating perfume, and a sensory engineer orchestrated the colors, textures, lighting, and sounds that made the cafe the romantic setting you needed to express your love.

Selecting a suit off the rack in a department store is similar to selecting a greeting card. Both meet your needs, but neither is custom tailored to your unique requirements. They are, however, based on cues and symbols that communicate to a large number of people. For example, restaurant designers who frequently produce romantic atmospheres know that the addition of such *universal cues* as a fireplace, soft lighting, soft colors, and music could transform even a barren bus terminal into a romantic setting.

Sensory engineers who specialize in creating private erotic spaces know that understanding *universal cues* is essential if they are to decode and channel an individual's unique erotic experiences and needs. This book illustrates many of the universal cues associated with romantic, seductive, and sensuous spaces. This chapter, in particular, will highlight such subtle cues as fragrances and lighting that create spatial ambience. Though you may not want to become a sensory engineer, your ability to recognize erotic cues will make your life more exciting.

The *erotic wheel* illustrates the concept of Eros (the center core) as the life-giving force that produces the psychic erotic energy necessary for the development of intimate relationships. Although the romantic, seductive, and sensuous space categories corresponding to intimate relationships are numbered on the wheel, *no one type dominates*. All three types of space are equally important in developing and sustaining healthy relation-

ships. The wheel further clarifies the continuous rhythmic movement between the different types of spaces. That is, as soon as intense psychic energy is released in the sensuous phase, our psychic batteries resume a recharging process at the romantic level.

The outer ring on the wheel has values of gray that show gradual increases in psychic energy evident in the three types of erotic spaces. (This can be compared with the diagram on page 15, which shows the levels of psychic energy needed to sustain evolving relationships.) The outer ring is also related to the color intensity associated with each type of space. For example, red may range from pale pinks in the romantic phase to intense vivid reds in the seductive phase and grow to deep rich reds in the sensuous phase. (This corresponds to the red values ranging from one to nine shown on the value scale on page 28.)

The universal cues listed below the wheel should be read from left to right to make further comparisons between the three types of spaces. The cues, which include moods, feelings, colors, forms, textures, music, fragrances, and temperatures, all reflect the psychic energy level of the particular erotic space. The subtle similarities between components on this list become evident. For example, just as color progresses from *soft* pastels to *intense vivid* colors to *rich deep* colors, temperatures also increase in intensity from *warm* to *simmering* to *boiling hot*. Further comparisons can be made with all the other universal cues on the chart.

The places included at the end of the list are those considered most supportive to evolving intimate relationships and therefore have become unconscious universal cues associated with the three space categories.

In order to show you how to recognize each type of erotic space, a sensory engineering chapter concludes each section. Chapters 5, 8, and 10 contain questionnaires, diagrams, tables, and charts that will serve as checklists to help you evaluate the erotic spaces shown in each of those sections.

The tree diagrams used throughout the book are based on the master chart shown at the right. This chart contains an overview of moods, feelings, and physical factors that contribute to particular erotic atmospheres.

When you study the romantic tree diagram (by reading from top to bottom), you will see that it categorizes the universal motivations and fantasies that make an environment romantic. For example, if a restaurant has a tropical islands theme it will be considered romantic by many people because it expresses the popular escape-to-an-exotic-faraway-place fantasy. There will be a more detailed discussion of the romantic diagram in Chapter 5.

Spaces, like people, are capable of projecting several images at the same time. In most cases that is more desirable than a space designed for only one mood. In each sensory engineering chapter the variety of romantic, seductive, or sensuous cues a space may contain will be listed in a table. An accompanying bar chart will visually illustrate the subtle differences. For example, romantic spaces are often easily identifiable because such romantic cues as soft colors and lighting dominate. Seductive spaces, however, tend to combine many romantic and sensuous cues and therefore offer a wider range of moods.

Before we move on to a detailed discussion of the three types of erotic spaces, we need to explore the general categories of universal sensory cues. Knowing the importance of fragrance,[1] color, sound, shape, form, texture, and lighting provides a backdrop against which the rest of the book is drawn.

[1]The section on fragrance that follows was based on material made available from the Fragrance Foundation and Naarden International. It directly correlates with the book's three categories of erotic spaces.

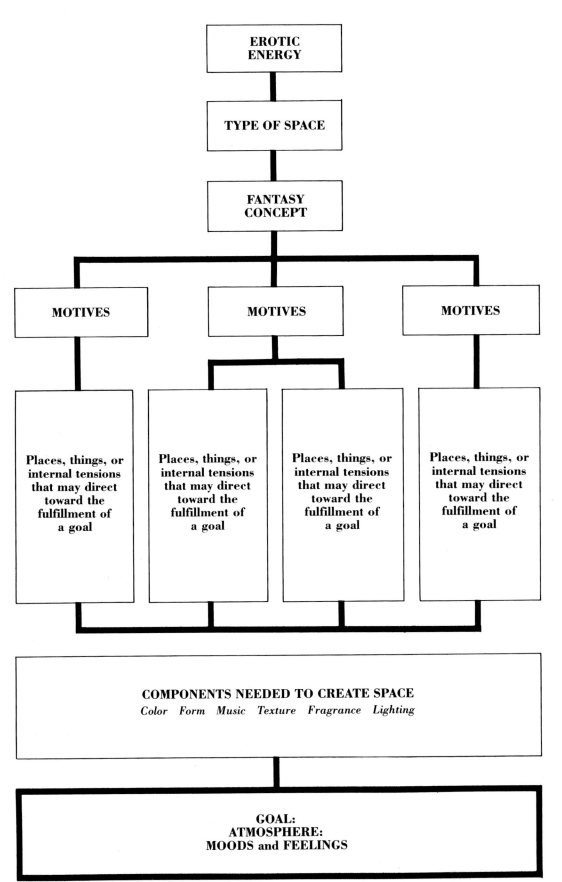

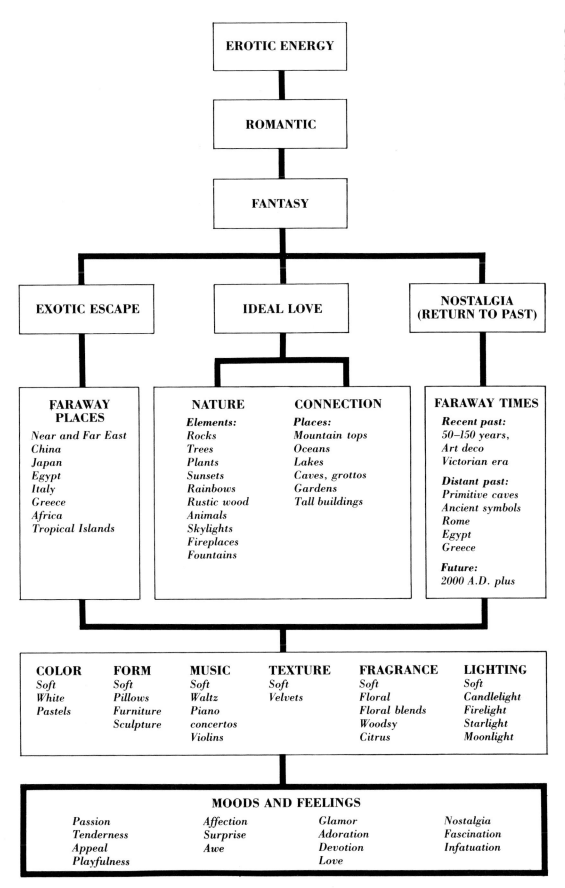

(Opposite page) Trace the many components needed to create an erotic atmosphere in the master tree diagram by reading from top to bottom. *(Left)* The romantic tree diagram lists *(from top to bottom)* the many ingredients needed to create a romantic environment.

EROTIC ENERGY

ROMANTIC

FANTASY

EXOTIC ESCAPE

IDEAL LOVE

NOSTALGIA (RETURN TO PAST)

FARAWAY PLACES

Near and Far East
China
Japan
Egypt
Italy
Greece
Africa
Tropical Islands

NATURE

Elements:
Rocks
Trees
Plants
Sunsets
Rainbows
Rustic wood
Animals
Skylights
Fireplaces
Fountains

CONNECTION

Places:
Mountain tops
Oceans
Lakes
Caves, grottos
Gardens
Tall buildings

FARAWAY TIMES

Recent past:
50–150 years,
Art deco
Victorian era

Distant past:
Primitive caves
Ancient symbols
Rome
Egypt
Greece

Future:
2000 A.D. plus

COLOR	**FORM**	**MUSIC**	**TEXTURE**	**FRAGRANCE**	**LIGHTING**
Soft	*Soft*	*Soft*	*Soft*	*Soft*	*Soft*
White	*Pillows*	*Waltz*	*Velvets*	*Floral*	*Candlelight*
Pastels	*Furniture*	*Piano*		*Floral blends*	*Firelight*
	Sculpture	*concertos*		*Woodsy*	*Starlight*
		Violins		*Citrus*	*Moonlight*

MOODS AND FEELINGS

Passion	*Affection*	*Glamor*	*Nostalgia*
Tenderness	*Surprise*	*Adoration*	*Fascination*
Appeal	*Awe*	*Devotion*	*Infatuation*
Playfulness		*Love*	

This table lists the romantic, seductive, and sensuous cues used to create romantic settings shown in Chapters 3 and 4.

ROMANTIC SETTINGS* Chapters 3 and 4	ROMANTIC ELEMENTS	SEDUCTIVE ELEMENTS	SENSUOUS ELEMENTS
1. Irresistible Beach House	Location: views Colors Fireplace	Mirrors	Spiral stairs
2. Skyline House	Location: views Surfaces: wood Skylights Fireplace		
3. The Coach House	Skylight Plants Nostalgia: art collection		
4. Inspired Echoes	Fireplace Nostalgia: faraway time and place (China) Plants		
5. Penthouse Panorama	Height: view Piano Art	Mirrors	
6. Magnificent Memories	Nostalgia: art deco Fireplace	Vivid colors Glittering fabrics	Furniture forms Sculpture
7. Lounging in Your Favorite Fantasy	Nostalgia: places, time, colors Ancient symbols: snakes	Furniture: lounges	
8. A Country Estate in Brooklyn	Nostalgia: time Plants Water: views		
9. Disco for a Pharaoh	Nostalgia: faraway places	Glittering lights Mirrors	Textures
10. A Lovers' Grotto Retreat	Nostalgia: time/rocks Symbols: animal forms Fireplace Location: view	Mirrors Animal fur Large spa Tusks	Furniture forms
11. A Desert Fantasy	Nostalgia: faraway time, place Colors Animals		
12. Exotic Chinese Bedroom	Nostalgia: faraway places, time (China) Fireplace Plants		

ROMANTIC SPACES*	ROMANTIC	SEDUCTIVE	SENSUOUS
Space 1	███████	▓▓▓▓▓	░░
Space 2	███████		
Space 3	███████		
Space 4	█████		
Space 5	███████	▓▓▓	
Space 6	███████	▓▓▓▓	
Space 7	███████	▓▓▓▓	
Space 8	██████		
Space 9	███████	▓▓▓▓	
Space 10	███████	▓▓▓▓	░░
Space 11	██████		
Space 12	███████		

The bar chart graphically illustrates the range of cues listed in the table on the opposite page.

Fragrance

Our response to most fragrances is based on memory, to things as simple as the smell of bread baking or coffee brewing. Most of these memories are linked to relationships with special people or places like home.

Fragrances designed for women have evolved into three dominant types: floral, Chrype, and Oriental (see diagram on page 23). Comparing them with the three types of erotic spaces shown on the erotic wheel (see page 16) reveals more than casual similarities. Floral is directly related to the concept of romantic spaces by the type of colors, textures, feelings, and moods provoked. The Chrype fragrances are very seductive. In its most simple form Chrype is composed of a crisp citrus combined with an oak moss. Its seductiveness comes from the wide range of responses it can evoke. The third type, Oriental, is the most sensuous, with an emphasis on depth and intensity.

As you survey the list of brand names in each of the categories you are probably able to pick out one or more fragrances that either you or someone you know has used over the years. By studying the categories from which most of your choices were made, you may be surprised to find that you choose consistently from the same groups, with the possible exception of perhaps one or two.

Compare the perfume category from which most of your choices were made with the erotic wheel. This should offer a clue about the type of space in which you may feel most comfortable. This does not mean that you must always seek out this type of environment, but it could help you determine the type of environment you will find yourself being drawn to time after time. Because our need for variety may at times necessitate all three types of interior spaces, our environments should be engineered to accommodate changes in mood, just as every fragrance is skillfully engineered to provoke a wide range of feeling.

The diagram on page 24 shows how fragrances are engineered. A triangle separated into three parts corresponds to what are known as "top, middle, and base notes." The top part provides the fresh lightness and sparkle of the fragrance, the middle note the

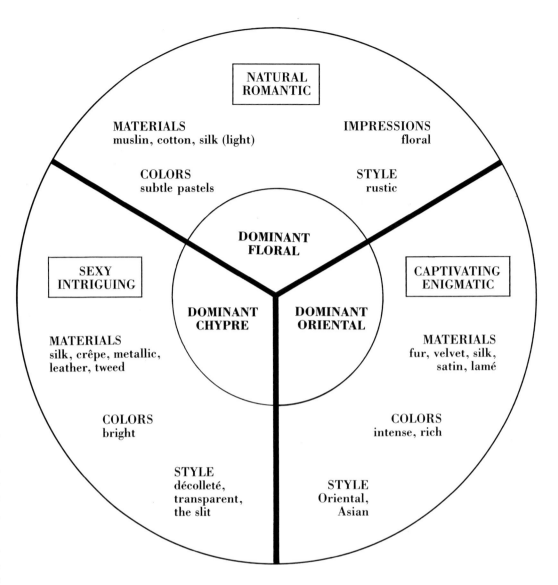

NATURAL ROMANTIC

MATERIALS
muslin, cotton, silk (light)

IMPRESSIONS
floral

COLORS
subtle pastels

STYLE
rustic

DOMINANT FLORAL

SEXY INTRIGUING

CAPTIVATING ENIGMATIC

DOMINANT CHYPRE

DOMINANT ORIENTAL

MATERIALS
silk, crêpe, metallic, leather, tweed

MATERIALS
fur, velvet, silk, satin, lamé

COLORS
bright

COLORS
intense, rich

STYLE
décolleté, transparent, the slit

STYLE
Oriental, Asian

FRAGRANCES		
ROMANTIC	**SEDUCTIVE**	**SENSUOUS**
FLORAL	**CHYPRE**	**ORIENTAL**
Natural Fragrances	*Oak Moss, Fruity, Woody, Spice*	*Sweet to Amber, Animal*
WOMEN		
Adolfo	*Aromatics*	*Alexandra*
Arpege	*Azuree*	*Bal a Versailles*
Calandre	*Bandit*	*Chanel #22*
Caleche	*Calvin Klein*	*Chantilly*
Chanel #5	*Cerissa*	*Charles of the Ritz*
Charlie	*Chamade*	*Cinnabar*
Chloe	*Chanel #19*	*Dioressence*
Enjoli	*Courreges*	*Galore*
Estee	*Galanos*	*Interlude*
First	*Givenchy III*	*K de Karza*
Gucci	*Halston*	*Kif*
Halston Night	*Mitsouko*	*Magie Noire*
Joy (Rose, jasmine)	*Nuit de Noel*	*Miss Dior*
Madame Rochas	*Tuxedo*	*Opium*
McFadden	*"Y"*	*Oscar de la Renta*
Missoni		*Pheromone-Miglin*
My Sin	**Green Citrus**	*Royal Secret*
Norell	*Armani*	*Senchal*
1000 de Patou	*Inoui*	*Shalimar*
Pavlova (Tuberose)	*Ivoire de Balmain*	*Tabu*
Tatiana (Gardenia)	*Lauren*	*Vanderbilt*
White Linen (Rose, jasmine)	*Metal*	*Youth Dew*
MEN		
Lavender Notes	**Woody Note**	
English Lavender	*English Leather*	
	Sandalwood	
	Vetiver	
	Chypre	
	Halston (Z-14/1-12)	
	Ice Blue Aqua Velva	
	Jade for Men	
	That Man	
	Spicy Note	
	Old Spice	
	Citrus Notes	
	English Leather	
	Green Note	
	Gray Flannel	
	Tabac Note	
	Kanon	
	Royal Copenhagen	

(Opposite page) The fragrance wheel, developed by Naarden International, has many similarities with the erotic wheel (see page 16). The dominant floral fragrance at the top of the diagram is associated with romantic cues such as soft materials, subtle soft colors, and a "rustic" style, which relates to the nature connection shown on the romantic tree diagram on page 18. If we move counter-clockwise, the dominant Chypre fragrances correspond to the seductive phase on the erotic wheel. The "sexy, intriguing" metallic materials, bright colors, and alluring décolleté slit add up to seduction. The dominant Oriental fragrances described as "captivating enigmatic" with rich, intense colors and satin fabrics correspond to the sensuous phase on the erotic wheel. The Oriental influence conjures up undulating forms such as swirling dragons and decorative cloud forms. (Left) Fragrance types and some of the more popular brand names in each category are listed above. Searching for your favorite fragrances will probably reveal that you have used the same general type repeatedly for many years. Male fragrances listed on the bottom half of this chart predominantly fall within the Chypre or seductive category, which corresponds to the male approach to intimate relationships.

personality and character or the aura the wearer wishes to project, and the base note the depth and length of time the fragrance will linger on the wearer.

The diagram on page 25 illustrates the color symbolism assigned to the various raw materials used to make a fragrance. The red line down the center represents the floral content found in all feminine perfumes. Florals are basically the middle notes, but they also play a role in the top and base notes. The citruses are the first of the top notes, and they also play a part in the formation of the middle notes, but their high-pitched notes are unable to function in the base. The green, fruity notes are used to give originality to a fragrance. Spices are found in all three notes; moss, wood, Oriental, animal, and amber notes fill out the base.

Notice the two other triangles drawn within the larger triangle. Each shape is varied to illustrate how a fragrance may vary. For example, the low, wide triangle with its emphasis on base notes will produce a sophisticated floral complex or a sensuous Oriental fragrance. The narrow inside triangle will produce a fragrance with emphasis on the fresh top notes.

All three parts of a fragrance are deeply intertwined. The same could be said of human relationships and corresponding romantic, seductive, and sensuous spaces. A disco with its highly stimulating seductive environment could be compared with a fragrance with only citrus top notes. Both the fragrance and the disco would have difficulty holding our interest for extended periods.

While the fragrances we wear appear to reflect our erotic energy level and are therefore important in understanding our spatial needs, the scented products we use in the home are equally vital to our well-being. Each time we wash the dishes, take a shower, or use scented toilet tissue, we are using a fragrance. Research about the types of fragrances used in the American home in the last twenty years has found that they have been primarily based on pine and citrus-lemon, which do not linger because they are top notes. More complex, sophisticated fragrances are being developed that will use a larger range of fragrance notes. Soon there may be many more complex fragrances to enhance your favorite erotic space.

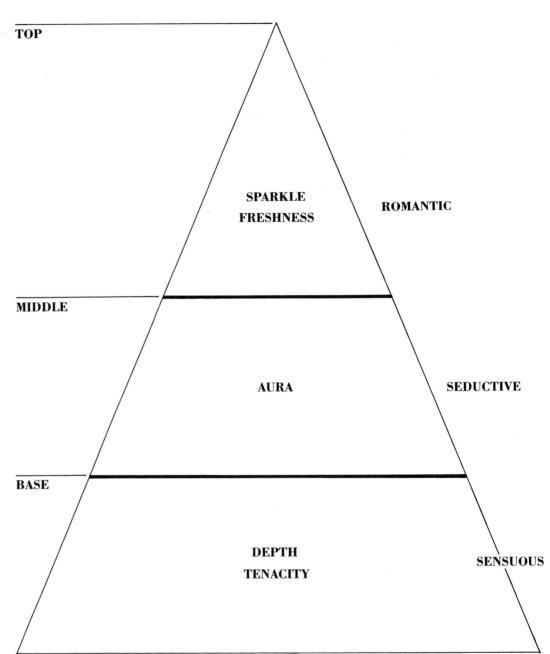

The diagram shows the three components that can be used in various combinations to create fragrances.

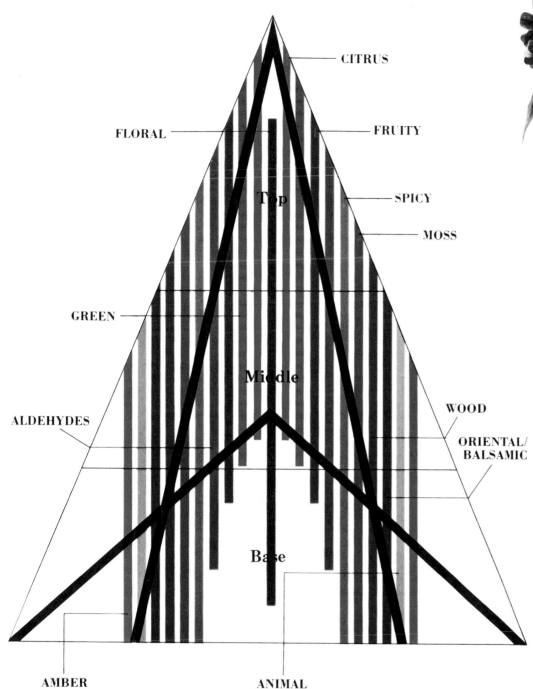

(Left) The fragrance color triangle, developed by Naarden International, closely parallels the author's findings about colors used in the three types of erotic spaces. This triangle is divided into three horizontal divisions: top, middle, and base, which roughly correspond to romantic, seductive, and sensuous fragrances. The ingredients used to make fragrances are referred to as "notes" and they are assigned symbolic colors on this triangle. For example, floral note (red) is basically a middle note and is part of all fragrances designed for women. Spicy notes (peach) are also found in all three levels of the triangle. The top note that represents floral fragrances contains a large proportion of citrus (yellow), green, and fruity (orange) elements. These particular notes do not extend below the middle or seductive section of the triangle. Fragrance components originating in this middle section are amber (turquoise), wood (brown), animal (gray), and Oriental/balsamic (deep red). The base of the triangle contains primarily those notes that give a deep lingering quality or tenacity to a fragrance. Sensuous fragrances require time to mellow as they are warmed by body temperature. (Above) Romantic, seductive, and sensuous visual cues are combined in this advertisement for Shalimar perfume by Guerlain. The male and female images projected by fragrances reveal many of our most cherished fantasies.

Pillows strewn around the floor set the stage for total abandon. The vertical phallic openings pointing toward the womblike opulence of the draped ceiling were symbols to drive men wild.

Sound

The influence of sounds in personal spaces is now acknowledged as a very important factor throughout our lives. Recently a physician discovered that babies slept better in a hospital nursery when they heard recordings of a woman's heartbeat combined with the fluid sounds from the womb. These sounds transferred to a small battery-operated instrument were installed inside a furry teddy bear, which has been marketed with great success.

We have developed "white" sound, similar to radio static, for the office, music is often broadcast in a wide variety of public places, and we spend thousands of dollars on music systems that can be operated from every inch of our personal erotic space. There are also devices that will lull you to sleep with the sounds of surf or rain. Though the speed of the surf can be controlled, it would be wise to proceed with caution when using the rain sounds. Don't repeat the failure of a woman attempting to create the perfect romantic atmosphere with the sound of rain; her lover

became alarmed and rushed out of the apartment to put up the windows on his automobile. Could you get serious about making love after that?

The sounds of music combined with the crackling of burning logs in the fireplace are a difficult duo to improve upon. Designing your erotic spaces to assure acoustic as well as visual privacy is a necessary part of sensory engineering.

The symbolism of shapes, forms, and textures

Symbols tend to develop spontaneously and become a type of secret language intuitively understood by what Jung described as the "collective unconscious."[2] We cover our bodies and our intimate environments with shapes and forms that are linked to highly charged ancient symbols. For example, though the clothes we wear and the automobile we drive represent very complex symbolism, both signal wealth and power.

The geometric shapes and forms in our environment have been used to symbolize all manner of eroticism dealing with female and male forms. Our earliest shelter, the rounded womblike cave, is part of the broad range of mother earth symbolism. The interiors of buildings and for that matter all enclosures or containers such as vases have been traditionally considered female symbols. Curvilinear shapes like the spiral and the serpent have frequently been portrayed as female symbols. The costume worn by Theda Bara in a 1920s movie shows the use of snake forms. The sofa shown in Royal Sensuality on page 161 illustrates the use of the typical serpentine form in furniture.

The circle links humanity to the cosmos and represents the wholeness of self. Therefore, it is easy to understand the popularity of the round bed and the round bean bag chair in spaces designed for bachelors. This further explains the impact of the round openings in the room shown on page 116.

[2]David Elkind, Ph.D., "Carl Jung," in Kaplan, Freedman, and Sadock, *Comprehensive Textbook of Psychiatry*, vol. 1, Baltimore, Md.: Williams and Wilkins Company, 1980, chap. 10.3, p. 813.

Vertical elements in our spaces such as pillars, columns, and doors can become phallic symbols. The setting shown on page 26 has an abundance of sexual symbolism. Phallic-shaped openings into the softly draped womblike ceiling of this room hold your attention. Phallic symbols are also incorporated into the lamps and various smoking paraphernalia.

Animal symbolism plays a large part in furniture designed for fantasy environments. The swan, the fish, the snake, and the feline have traditionally been associated with the female and are frequently found incorporated into highly eroticized furnishings. The bull, the lion, as well as elephant tusks have been symbols of masculine verility and strength. The powerful tusks shown on page 117 illustrate the forcefulness of these shapes.

You have probably noted on the erotic wheel that textures in all three types of interiors range from soft to smooth. Actual materials are those that encourage stroking, such as fur, feathers, suede, soft leathers, and velvets. The combination of smooth and shiny is particularly erotic. The bedroom on page 102 in Chapter 7 is a typical example of this combination. The rocks used in the lovers' grotto shown on pages 62–64 in Chapter 4 are also part of the texture that may be found in an erotic space.

Careful attention should be paid to every symbolic detail of this seduction scene. Theda Bara is lavishly covered in ancient animal symbols that portray her power. The snake forms coiled around her breasts and arms and poised on her forehead were meant to seduce the big-game hunter fantasy lurking in men.

Color

We are heavily influenced by colors on four different levels. On the physiological level color can affect our pulse rate and physical responses. On the social level our associations are based on prevailing styles, fashions, and traditional attitudes, such as blue for boys and pink for girls. The emotional and sensory levels are instinctive and difficult to distinguish from the fourth level that is related to personal associations and memories.[3]

It is interesting to note that the fragrance industry relates color with the fragrances they produce and that their color concepts are closely linked to those used in interior spaces.

Although individual color preferences vary widely, when asked to relate particular colors to erotic spaces, most people qualify their selection by emphasizing the color *intensity*. For example, most people associate pastels—that is, light, soft tints—with romantic environments. Therefore, on a typical value scale, the pastels, or values one through three, function as universal cues in romantic spaces. All colors that extend from one to nine on the value scale can be used in erotic spaces. Yellow, however, is the only color that cannot move up and down the scale. It corresponds to the citrus top note on the fragrance triangle and, as in fragrance, cannot function in all three types of erotic spaces. Therefore yellow is usually found in erotic settings only when it is combined with

[3]Robert M. Goldberg, Ph.D., *The Encyclopedia of Human Behavior: Psychology, Psychiatry, and Mental Health*, vol. 1, Garden City, N.Y.: Doubleday and Company, 1970, pp. 228–229.

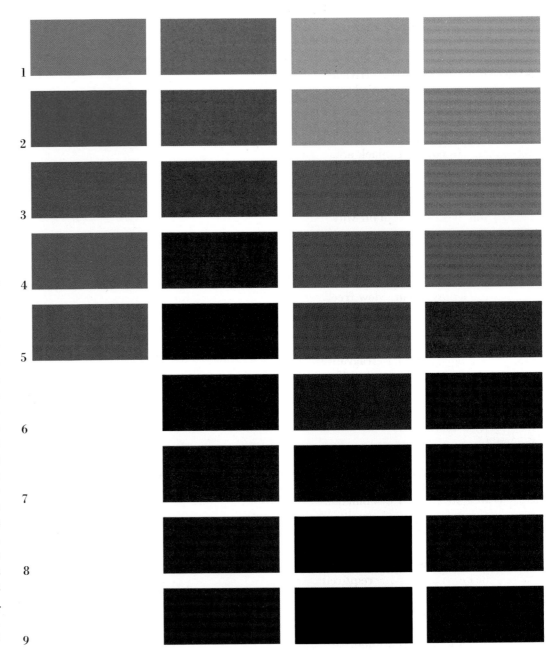

The color value scale provides a means of describing the intensity of a color. For example, red with the addition of white becomes a tint (pink) (1). When mixed with either black or its complimentary hue the intensity of red can be decreased or lowered on the value scale (9). All hues or colors are capable of a wide value range, with the exception of yellow. Note that when black is added to yellow it will change to green. It is therefore a high-pitched color that could be compared with the citrus top note on the fragrance triangle because it lacks the depth and intensity to function in some sensuous spaces.

another color, for example, when mixed with red to produce orange.

Black and white, officially noncolors, are also associated with erotic environments. The association is frequently tied to a texture or an animal image; that is, a soft, fluffy white cat is considered very romantic, and of course, romantic heroes always rode on white horses. In contrast, black animals are associated with seductive and sensuous qualities and, generally, with evil. The black panther and black stallion fit the description. Perhaps this begins to explain why women traditionally wear white on romantic occasions and black lace when wishing to project a very seductive or sensuous mood.

To understand the use of color in sensory engineering, let your mind flow freely while thinking about the various universal sensory cues. Let images surface, and play with them. For example, if you begin associating colors with music, temperatures, fragrance, and textures, you will soon find yourself thinking like a sensory engineer.

Lighting

We may use many seemingly strange light sources in erotic interiors that would never be acceptable in other environments. Since erotic environments do not normally demand a high light level, we are free to use moonlight, starlight, candlelight, sunlight, firelight, or even the light from fireflies, if it supplies the mood and feeling required. Skylights are a wonderful source of natural daylight and moonlight. They can be installed directly over a dining area or over a bed for romantic moments under the stars. The drawings above illustrate the many angles and sizes that might meet your needs.

Of course, electric light is also available. Some sensory engineers specialize in lighting that will meet the specific requirements of romantic, seductive, and sensuous spaces. On this and the next page basic types of installations are shown that range from recessed and ceiling-mounted tracks to wall-mounted and floor-standing types of lighting. For example, an excellent way to obtain general soft lighting for a romantic space is to use a wall sconce or a tall floor lamp designed to direct light to the ceiling. Specific spot lights

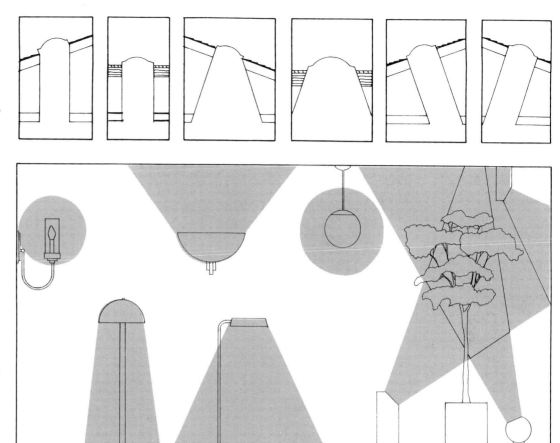

(Top) Skylights can take many forms and admit light from many different angles. Whether you desire moonlight and starlight over your bed or dancing sunlight over your breakfast table, a skylight can create many special effects in your erotic space.

(Above) Before making decisions about lamps or lighting equipment for your sensuous spaces, remember to determine what you want to highlight or backlight or where you want to cast mysterious shadows. This drawing illustrates the various directions that lamps can throw light to create a romantic, seductive, or sensuous mood.

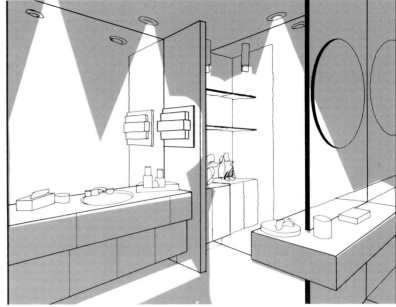

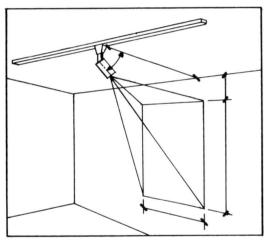

Lighting Data for Framing Projector

MAXIMUM LIGHT COVERAGE ON WALL AT TYPICAL AIMING ANGLES OF 36°, 45°, AND 60° FROM HORIZONTAL WITH SHUTTERS FULLY OPEN

EXAMPLE:

Problem: Where should the framing projector be mounted to light an 18″ × 36″ painting which is 30″ down from the ceiling?

Solution: Mount the track 24″ from the picture. At an aiming angle of 60° (the optimum for lighting pictures), the framing projector will light an area 24″ wide by 62″ high, 26″ down from the ceiling. The lighted area can then be reduced to the size of the painting with the shutters.

DISTANCE (D)	**24″**	**36″**
AIMING ANGLE (A) (from horizontal)	30° 45° 60°	30° 45° 60°
DISTANCE (C) (Min.)	11″ 18″ 26″	12″ 23″ 36″
WIDTH (W) (Max.)	18″ 20″ 24″	28″ 31″ 36″
LENGTH (L) (Max.)	26″ 34″ 62″	40″ 52″ 94″

(Above left) A bath created by designer James Callahan illustrates how a space can be erotically lit to provide task as well as soft background lighting. (Photo: Sheldon Lettich) (Above) An analysis of the lighting in the bath shows how light sources were recessed in the ceiling and under countertops as well as attached to walls to cast lighting in diverse direc-

tions. Each light source serves a particular function in creating the total mood of the room. (Left) Precious art work, a plant, or any object you wish can be highlighted with an exact amount of light by using a framing projector. The accompanying chart developed by Lightolier provides the distances and aiming angles needed for the desired placement of the fixture.

called "framing projectors" provide the maximum amount of light to correctly spotlight a painting, sculpture, or plants, often the focal point of an erotic space. The aiming angles vary, for instance, according to the light's distance from the painting and the size of the painting. A number of variations are shown on the accompanying chart.

Successful lighting creates a desired mood without anyone being aware of its presence, while lighting that is obvious and calls attention to the light source is distracting. Although track lighting was originally designed for ease in adjusting individual fixtures, it is frequently used in situations that are not suitable for track installations. For example, in a very small apartment living room the angle of the fixtures may make the light shine directly into people's eyes as they enter the

space. As you look at the various types of erotic spaces in this book, try to determine the light sources. Are they located at floor level, throwing light upward, or recessed into the ceiling? Most successful erotic spaces have devices that can regulate lighting levels depending on the required atmosphere. The bath shown above illustrates how several types of lighting can be successfully combined to create an exciting, glamorous setting. The lighting analysis points out the subtle use of lighting recessed under cabinets. This is combined with skillfully controlled down lighting.

Now that you have a general perspective on erotic spaces, you are ready to discover the many facets of entry-level romantic settings. Part 2 delves into the various types of fantasy that come alive in romantic spaces.

PART TWO

ROMANTIC INTERIORS

3

In Search of the Romantic

Entry-level erotic spaces are those that nurture the beginning phases of human relationships. These romantic spaces create a cocoonlike suspension from reality that allows two people to get to know each other and to measure their new love against their idealized image of love. Romantic spaces encourage relationships to deepen and mature, thus allowing lovers to release long-hidden fantasies, hopes, dreams.

In a natural sequence people eventually emerge from this romantic cocoon to cope with the realities of everyday living. But memories of that romantic suspension from reality urge us to recapture that idealized state of love by returning to romantic spaces. If fact, reclaiming lost romance appears to have become an urgent national preoccupation of the eighties.

In addition to memorable people and events, the search for the romantic involves special places or settings. While romantic events can happen on a street corner, favorite romantic settings usually have soft colors, soft lighting, soft textures, soft music, intimacy, coziness, and warmth.

No one seems to mind that this tree is made from stone and metal. The holiday mood created by the twinkling lights, the glowing pinks, and the nostalgic Victorian-style furnishings spell romance to thousands who travel to this restaurant at Madonna Inn. (Photo: © Russell Abraham)

What makes a setting romantic?

Romantic settings are shaped by the yearning to find an ideal partner. That search leads us into closer contact with nature. We can further suspend reality by escaping to faraway times and places.

Nature Connection. Finding a remote and secluded place means getting in touch with nature. Traveling to the edge of the ocean, a lake, or the top of a mountain offers inspiring views of water, landscapes, mist, fog, rainbows, and sunsets. This nature connection is so powerful that we create settings to resemble them. Though not remote or secluded, penthouses provide a mountainlike vista, or people occasionally choose to have dinner in a sophisticated restaurant at the top of a tall building.

Whenever culture is on the brink of a romantic revival this link with nature intensifies. In the late seventies and early eighties, amidst sleek high-tech interiors, designers began filling spaces with trees and plants. The lobby of the Westin Crown Center Hotel in Kansas City is an example. The five-story waterfall built of natural limestone creates a powerful romantic setting that would be difficult to resist, whether on a honeymoon or a business trip. America is filled with hotels, plazas, and shopping malls that bear a distinct similarity to the Crystal Palace built in England at the peak of the romantic Victorian era over 130 years ago.

Nostalgia for Another Time or Era. A sense of nostalgia is another theme of romantic places. Restaurant owners have long understood the importance of establishing a link with the past, a sense of déjà vu. For example, the all-pink Victorian-style dining room at the Madonna Inn in California combines nature with the charm of another era. The metal branches of a huge artificial tree are adorned with candelabra and twinkling lights that create a glamorous romantic mood. Convinced that pink is the ultimate romantic color, the owner of the inn compliments each meal with pink bread.

Less dramatic, but equally nostalgic, the restaurant on page 35 evokes a quaint country garden effect with many plants, trellis walls, and a skylight. When compared with the Victorian conservatory shown in a French painting of the nineteenth century it is further evidence that our ideas about romantic settings have changed very little over the last 150 years.

Exotic Escapes. Exotic spaces, usually combining nostalgia for another era with the mystery of another culture, are another type of romantic space. The interior of the Coconut Grove Restaurant, photographed in 1946, transported diners to another time and place. Moorish architectural details set among palm trees created an exotic fantasy from the Arabian Nights. In fact, very few successful restaurants in America lack a touch of fantasy. Numerous types of exotic settings in hotels, restaurants, bars, and homes are shown in Chapter 4.

Once we have found a romantic setting with natural beauty and nostalgic links to faraway times and places, we want to experience it with someone special. Sharing romantic spaces helps us develop and sustain intimate relationships. The spaces shown in the remainder of this chapter contain all the romantic qualities needed to become settings for magnificent obsessions.

(Opposite page left) Incorporating nature into buildings became popular during the peak of the Victorian period. The Crystal Palace, an English exhibition center built in 1851, was a glass and steel structure built around large trees on the site. (Opposite page top right) Built around a natural rocky formation, this four-story waterfall in the Kansas City Westin Crown Hotel is an excellent example of bringing nature into the built environment during this contemporary era of romantic revival. (Opposite page bottom right) Typical of many large hotels built during the late 70s and early 80s, the large atrium of the Hyatt Hotel in Washington, D.C., bears a strong resemblance to the Crystal Palace. (Left) This Victorian conservatory could easily be mistaken for the restaurant below or, for that matter, many American restaurants designed in the eighties. Our romantic concepts appear to change very little from one century to another. (Below left) This charming nostalgic restaurant designed by David S. Miller contains outstanding romantic cues. The trees, trellis, and skylight create a gardenlike setting. (Below) The popularity of many restaurants may be attributed to a timeless romantic theme that transports diners to a faraway erotic land. The 1946 Coconut Grove Restaurant, for instance, used an Arabian Nights theme. (Photo: Bison Archives)

Irresistible beach house

This hideaway is within easy driving distance from a married couple's townhouse. Totally different from their daily environment, the setting designed by Edward Turrentine and Jennifer Bevan, allows them to frequently rekindle the spark of romance in their marriage.

As one approaches the living room from the small secluded courtyard the vista begins to expand. The openness of the wide spiral stair serves to enhance it. All the interior space is kept low-keyed so that the beach, ocean, and sky can cast their spell on all who enter. The wooden floors and ceilings were bleached a light sand color. The upholstery fabrics are also kept light in color and feeling. The dining area set to one side of the living area is furnished with a large light acrylic table that does not obstruct the view of the ocean. Tall glass doors open directly onto a deck used for entertaining or watching the moonlight on the water. Louvered shutters provide privacy on the beach side of the living room.

The second floor bedroom includes every detail that could possibly be needed to promote romance—a fireplace, a view of the sea, and mirrors. The windows are arched and slightly vaulted to give added drama to the room. Two walls are mirrored to reflect beautiful ocean sunsets from all vantage points. The fourth wall contains a fireplace that can be used as needed to take the chill from the evening air. Even though the room is shared by a man and a woman, the bed covered in a delicate floral pattern and lightly trimmed in lace appears entirely appropriate. Not overpowering, the bed's subtle message clings to our memory like a beloved fragrance.

(Opposite page left) Designers Edward Turrentine and Jennifer Bevan bleached the wooden floors and ceilings a sand color and kept everything in the living area low keyed to allow the ocean to dominate the view. (Opposite page right) The delicate floral pattern trimmed in lace that covers the bed in the master bedroom does not project an overwhelmingly feminine feeling for two people secure in their love. (Above) Tall glass doors open directly onto a deck from the dining and living areas. A large acrylic table is surrounded by chairs upholstered in pale sand-colored silk appliqued with subtle shell motifs. (Right) As one approaches the living room from this small romantic courtyard the vista begins to expand. (Photos: David Glomb)

Skyline house

The big skyline house is built on a hill in the middle of a field overlooking a distant lake and fog-shrouded hills. This house serves as a second home for its designer Agnes Bourne and therefore fulfills that romantic craving for nature and the need to withdraw from the crowded city. Built of old weathered boards, with windows carefully placed to catch the breezes that sweep in low from the canyon, this house dominates the skyline. While large exposed trusses act as visual arms holding the house to the field, porches resembling waterfront docks seem to float on the summer grasses.

Reused materials also make the interior spaces glow with a variety of textures and colors. At the center of the house/barn is a huge fireplace that opens to both the living room and dining/kitchen area. It serves as the hub of activities and is responsible for the warm, cozy feeling that permeates the entire home.

The large, open spaces in the main area of the house are used for painting and music studios. A loft provides additional work space and sleeping areas. Large skylights are carefully placed to catch both day and night light. In the main bedroom a skylight was purposely positioned over the bed to catch the light of the moon as it moves across the sky. As the moon journeys beyond this skylight it can be seen in the early morning hours from one in the studio.

Romantics to the core, and not shy about letting the world know it, the designer-owners were well aware of the erotic psychic energy levels needed in their environment.

(Top) A carefully positioned skylight over the bed in the master bedroom allows the moon to be viewed as it travels across the heavens. (Above) The house sits atop a hill overlooking a distant lake and fog-shrouded hills. Designed by Agnes Bourne, the house is positioned to catch the breezes that sweep in low from the canyon. (Opposite page) The glowing fireplace produces a cozy romantic feeling throughout the living-dining and kitchen areas. It becomes the hub of all activities. (Photos: Ron Super)

Magnificent memories

The outrageous eroticism and decadent vulgarity of the twenties have become high romance in the eighties as our smooth reentry into this time warp is expertly executed by designer Dennis Abbé.

In this apartment aglow with nostalgic colors, forms, and textures, you will find fragments of columns from buildings, now part of our collective architectural memory, interwoven with objects that stir very personal connections. Furnishings that your mother or grandmother may have onced owned appear strangely familiar here.

The entry area is softly illuminated by beams of light directed upward from floor-standing lamps. A rich deep red on the walls and sofa is contrasted with the glimmer of fabrics woven with silver and gold. Opposite walls of the living room are accented with large black triangular mirrors framed in copper. On either side of the mirror stand black lacquered torcheres that were cast from columns found in the Florence Ziegfield Theater built in New York City in the 1920s.

Over the marble mantel a three-piece mirror with matching wall sconces doubles the enjoyment of the space. The art deco chandelier reflected in the mirror forms an exotic background for the sensuous female nude sculpture by Joe Descompas. To the right is a lacquered bronze cup by Jean Durand, and on the left is a turquoise Schneider vase made in 1925. In the fireplace below is a gracefully carved capital from a wooden pilaster that once adorned the walls of the famed Roxy movie theater. Amidst all the artifacts from the past, a fresh floral arrangement near the fireplace appears to have been preserved for over fifty years. The bedroom, though more Edwardian in style, repeats the same sensuous colors and textures used in the living room area.

The designer-owner of this apartment enjoys being surrounded by everything from this extravagant time. To further preserve the magnificent memories of those Abbé calls "unrepentant sinners and lovers of beauty," he often dresses for dinner in a 1920s tuxedo.

(Top left) The New York apartment designed by Dennis Abbé recreates the opulent art deco period. The entry is softly illuminated by beams of light directed to the ceiling by floor-standing torcheres. (Top right) The bedroom walls are hand painted with scrolled borders and marblized textures on the woodwork. The same intense reds used in the living room are combined with the rich glow of brass. (Above) Another sensuous stylized female nude sculpture accents the marble fireplace. (Right) The disciplined and highly stylized eroticism of the 20s is captured in this bronze sculpture of a female archer. (Opposite page) On one living room wall a large black triangular mirror is flanked on either side with large black lacquered torchere columns. The gleaming gold- and silver-type fabric used on the chairs was typical of the period. (Photos: Robert Bonifield)

Inspired echoes

Interior spaces that provided the settings for the romance and marriage of Delores Costello and John Barrymore inspired the refurbishing of this space. It is rumored that during prohibition this 57-foot space was once used as a ballroom. The third-floor location and lowered ceilings could apparently provide the privacy required for serving forbidden liquor to large parties.

To create a romantic hideaway for today's use, Douglas Pierce Hiatt partially divided the long space into three sections by portieres. One end is very casually furnished with wicker and Oriental accents. This adjoins an elegant central lounging area with soft voluptuously upholstered seating that surrounds a small fireplace.

Beyond the second portiere on a slightly raised platform is the sleeping area. An enormous Oriental bed fills the entire space. Large Buddha-head vases filled with exotic blossoms flank each side of the bed. The walls are covered in a subtle Oriental print. Carefully placed lighting creates soft patterns on the floor and adds romantic shadows on the ceilings.

(Top right) Douglas Pierce Hiatt refurbished spaces that once served as settings for John Barrymore's lavish parties. This long space with low ceilings was furnished casually and divided into three areas with portieres. (Right) A rare Oriental bed flanked on either side with large Buddha-head vases fills the entire bedroom area. Soft lighting casts romantic shadows on the ceiling.

The coach house

This very romantic space designed by Bruce Goers was once an old coach house in the suburbs of Chicago. The space, formerly an attic bedroom for the chauffeur, was cleared of partitions, and one grand room was created for sleeping and entertaining. The soaring skylight admits sunlight across the room and, of course, moonlight and starlight. The owner compares the space with a tree house.

Many romantic settings have skylights that create a link with nature and open the space above. For centuries religious architecture has successfully expressed the idea that something inspirational happens when viewing a soaring architectural element. It is the same feeling evoked when looking up into a tall pine tree or standing at the bottom of a cliff. It is a consciousness-raising experience, in that we are made aware of the vastness of the universe and our part within nature's network.

The crocodile bench from New Guinea and the statue of a saint that was used in the filming of "The Agony and the Ecstasy" reveal a romantic interest in things from the past and objects collected from faraway places.

(Above) Exotic fantasies are expressed in the sculpture and crocodile bench collected from faraway places. Although this environment renovated by Bruce Goers encompasses only one room, it contains items that continually expand the imagination. (Right) This coach house features a soaring skylight that opens a large portion of the area to the stars and moon. Daylight is controlled by a movable bamboo shade. (Photos: David Glomb)

Penthouse panorama

This penthouse high above Manhattan has many qualities that could be described as romantic, but it is seductive and sensuous as well. Unlike many other well-designed spaces that depend primarily on lighting controls to vary the mood, this penthouse displays versatility through its spatial arrangements and its contents designed by Tom Foerderer. For example, romance is sensed from the moment you enter by turn-of-the-century art lining the wall of the entry gallery. Also notice the double forces that are at work near the far end of this space. A baby grand piano, one of the romantic musical symbols of this century, is placed in front of an otherwise unobstructed view of the world below.

Sensing that the dining area might be over-powered, the designer added emphasis to the custom-built seating and circular travertine dining table by repeating the forms in a ceiling soffit.

The living room, located just beyond and to the right of the dining area, is small and intimate. Custom-built banquettes line two walls. A third wall is covered with mirrors and slides from view to make the living room an extension of the bedroom.

The most serene areas in this home are the bedroom and bath. Windows on two sides provide a spectacular view of the city. Rather than repeat the skyline in a mirrored wall, the designer chose to reflect it in the shiny laminate surface of a storage wall. A custom-built lounging area under the far window is covered in raw silk to match the bed and all other upholstered pieces in the penthouse.

Travertine marble and black laminate cover almost all surfaces in the bath. A large shower replaced a tub, and long counters provide a luxurious dressing area for two.

To compensate for placing the kitchen in the center core, the designer used many reflective surfaces. Shiny black laminate trimmed with aluminum strips and combined with mirrors and lighting adds sparkle and a sense of seduction to an area that might otherwise have been uninteresting.

The use of low-keyed colors such as gray, beige, and silver punctuated with black creates a subtle background for nurturing romance.

(Opposite page) A Manhattan penthouse designed by the late Tom Foerderer projects unmistakable romance through the use of 19th-century posters, a magnificient baby grand piano, and a commanding view of the city below. (Far left) The kitchen of this penthouse is designed in black laminate trimmed with aluminum strips. This is combined with mirrors and sparkling lights to transform a mundane area into sleek and sensuous space. (Left) Luxurious travertine marble covering the shower walls and counter tops is combined with the same black laminate used in the kitchen to create a very elegant type of romantic sensuality. (Below) A custom-built lounging area under the window at the far end of the bedroom is a perfect romantic spot for late evening lounging. (Photos: Mark Ross)

A romantic tradition: the honeymoon setting

The honeymoon is one of the most special romantic occasions traditionally set aside for those madly in love couples known as newlyweds. Although honeymoons have a long tradition, they are not what they used to be. Today many couples view the honeymoon as a means of recharging their erotic energy level and therefore take honeymoons as frequently as they replace the batteries in their radios.

The tradition began with the combination of the two words "honey" and "moon." Heavily weighted with sexual meanings, these words were first used together some time in the fifteenth century. Their combination represented a perceptive understanding of how intimate relationships evolve.

When honey was discovered in ancient times it almost immediately became linked to fertility, love, and marriage. The ancient sweetener was also considered an aphrodisiac and even thought to have magical powers. For example, in India the groom was frequently given a jar of honey with wishes that the marriage be sweet, fruitful, and good, and the bride was covered with honey to make a sticky, but assuredly sweet wedding night.

The moon was also linked to fertility and extolled in poetry and songs for centuries. The ancients understood that as the spring changes to summer and a full moon wanes within a month's time, the intense heat of new love evolves into a more stable, secure relationship. By linking the moon with honey they were to remind us forever that the first month after marriage should be set aside to savor the sweetness of that new relationship.

From the middle ages to the mid-nineteenth century, it was customary at both royal and nonroyal weddings for guests to lead the bride and groom into the bedchamber. This traditional bedding down of the couple symbolized that the union was consummated. To make sure that this took place the bride and the groom were assisted in undressing by their respective attendants. When both were in bed, the celebration would continue in the bedchamber as the bride tossed her stocking (not yet flowers) to be caught by some lucky person. The guests would not leave until the local priest arrived to bless the newlyweds in their bedchamber.

Newlyweds have traditionally picked honeymoon settings that are eroticized. Typical choices have been the seaside, mountain tops, waterfalls, and faraway places such as tropical islands, historic cities, or places steeped in nostalgia. The hotels and lodges that have welcomed newlyweds had quiet rooms with a view, a fireplace, and lots of privacy. They also provided a dining room with soft music and secluded nooks, plus speedy room service for those who decided not to be seen at all. A healthy respect for the "do not disturb" sign was also the hallmark of a successful honeymoon hotel.

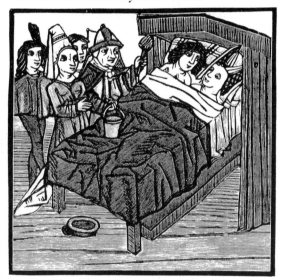

In the fifteenth century the wedding night was a family and community affair. The ceremony was completed only after the local priest blessed the consummation. (Drawing: Fuchs)

For three decades the best known and most popular "honeymoon capital" in America—Niagara Falls, New York—had all the necessary romantic ingredients of a breathtaking waterfall and quiet hotels. Although this natural wonder still attracts approximately 5 million visitors a year, only about 5 percent are newlyweds. In the early 1980s city officials began a search for the oldest couple who spent their honeymoon there and planned to offer them a return trip in order to regain national visibility as a honeymoon setting.

Even though people still seek out romantic locations, our shifting cultural attitudes and lifestyles prompted by the Sexual Revolution are forcing dramatic changes in hotel and resort facilities. The honeymoon, which only a generation ago provided the privacy and seclusion needed for the consummation of the marriage, hardly seems necessary in a society where the majority of couples have lived together for varying periods of time before getting married. For many newlyweds the honeymoon now takes on the character of an opulent vacation, a celebration of their chosen commitment to each other. Thus these first honeymoons essentially serve the same purpose as a second honeymoon, that is, a time to renew that old spark. Many resorts and private beach clubs have been established to cater to this new breed of honeymoon couple. Recreational activities are planned for both day and evening hours and usually include swimming, fishing, tennis, horseback riding, skiing, and socializing with other couples.

Even hotels that do not cater exclusively to newlyweds have begun to reflect this trend. Many no longer have separate honeymoon suites, but design a large percentage of rooms with huge bath tubs and oversized beds usually found only in traditional honeymoon settings. The playboy bachelor pad concept has also been adapted by hotels to entice newlywed couples who wish to revive the physical attraction grown dull during premarital living arrangements. Round beds, mirrored ceilings, furlike bedspreads, closed circuit movies, and other erotic stimuli lend excitement to the honeymoon.

Currently favored American honeymoon spots include ski resorts and mountain retreats. A group of ten resorts located in eastern Pennsylvania's Pocono Mountains host about 300,000 newlyweds each year. Famous for their heart-shaped bathtubs for two, four-poster white ruffled tester beds, and fireplaces, the Pocono resorts offer a moderately priced honeymoon package. They provide both indoor and outdoor sports in the summer and winter. Like many other honeymoon resorts, they also have the glamor of disco nightlife.

European-style accommodations based on the bed-and-breakfast concept have broadened the choices available as honeymoon set-

(Left) Pocono honeymoon cabins are equipped with such typical American romantic symbols as heart-shaped bath tubs, maple four-poster beds with white ruffled canopies, wood-burning fireplaces, and televisions.

(Below) The restored Spreckles Mansion in San Francisco offers bed-and-breakfast lodging often chosen by honeymooners who particularly enjoy candlelit fireside baths in an authentic claw-foot tub. (Photo: © Russell Abraham)

tings in the United States. For example, the Spreckels Mansion built in 1887 in San Francisco can offer newlyweds a Victorian fantasy in one of the most romantic cities in the world.

How would you like to become Scarlett O'Hara and Rhett Butler, acting out your magnificent love scenes against "Gone with the Wind" settings? The resident owners of the Nottoway Plantation overlooking the Mississippi River near Baton Rouge, Louisiana, offer bed-and-breakfast accommodations to visitors. Newlyweds are frequently seen strolling about the grounds and through rooms filled with memories of honeymoons long past. Large floor-to-ceiling windows open to verandas that give a view of the river beyond the levee. Knowing that your canopied wedding bed has been in this home for over a hundred years should enhance your honeymoon fantasy.

(Above) This bedroom, like the rest of the Nottoway Plantation, is furnished with objects purchased prior to the Civil War. (Right) The front veranda and the Mississippi River can be seen from the large windows of the plantation ballroom. (Opposite page) Attracted to the nostalgia of another time, newlyweds frequently stroll the grounds of the romantic plantation near Baton Rouge. (Louisiana Office of Tourism)

Escape into the Exotic

Romance and fantasy are synonymous. We cloth our erotic desires in romantic idealization and sublimation while disguising unconscious wishes in ancient symbols. Fantasies offer a means of wish fulfillment and promise a solution to personal conflicts. The Cinderella story is a classic example of romantic fantasy because the prince finds his ideal love and Cinderella is able to escape her otherwise cruel fate.

Popular childhood fairy tales have become incorporated into our storehouse of fantasies that are usually interrupted by adult responsibilities. Fantasies may linger just below the surface for years waiting to be fulfilled. Given the opportunity, these denied fantasies will quickly reappear and demand top priority in our lives. For example, a designer related the story of a recently widowed woman who spent a large sum of money refurbishing a new penthouse. Though the bedroom she had shared with her husband for thirty years had been a classic, tailored space, she wanted her new bedroom to be finished in ruffles and lace.

During the 1983 winter baseball training camp of the Chicago Cubs a select group of business and professional men, ranging in ages from thirty-three to sixty-three, paid sizable sums of money to spend a week with

This scene from a 1920s movie incorporates many of the classic symbols of our favorite fantasies. (Photo: Bison Archives)

their childhood idols. The fantasy week culminated with a 15-inning game between the Cubs and their guests. "It's been a lifetime dream. I have never had so much fun in my life," exclaimed one of the guests, who happened to be a practicing psychiatrist. "I don't know how we're going to get back to reality."

Getting in touch with your fantasies

Our relationships with others are partially based on three major types of socially motivated fantasies, namely, power, sex, and love. If you want to determine your major fantasies start by ranking the following list of motives according to their importance in your life (1 = most important; 10 = least important):

__ Prestige	__ Recognition (fame)
__ Love	
__ Sexual conquest	__ Social acceptance
__ Possessions	__ Success (career)
__ Physical attractiveness	
	__ Status
	__ Money

Ranking money, success, status, prestige, and fame as top priority could mean you are

a person driven by power fantasies. If love, physical attractiveness, and social acceptance top your list, your fantasies are based on love. If sexual conquest is your top priority, then sex is your driving force.

Based on the old cliche that "actions speak louder than words," compare your answers to the following questions with the priority list you just completed.

1. What magazines do you subscribe to?

2. What automobiles do you drive or would you like to own?

3. How many evenings this week did you spend working overtime?

4. How many brief sexual encounters did you have in the past year?

5. What types of aphrodisiacs did you use this week? (See Chapter 8 for more about aphrodisiacs.)

Fantasies can and do involve everything we do, everything we own, the places we frequent, the food we eat, and even the magazines we read. For example, someone who reads *Fortune, Business Week,* and *The Wall Street Journal* would appear to be seriously concerned about power, that is, money, career, status, recognition, and fame. If *Playboy* and *Cosmopolitan* are added to the list, the fantasy motives would have to be expanded to include sexual conquests.

Sleek European sport cars are associated with sexual conquest and power (which

(Right) Since our bedrooms are filled with fragments of fantasies, displaying these figures in a bedroom seems entirely appropriate. The mother and child constructed of blue sky and clouds seem out of touch with the more worldly "perfect Child" that reaches out to them. In the foreground a "lady of the house" attempts to break away from an image she detests, while a computer-headed man looks on. Although his arm has been lost in hard-fought battles, his computerized mind still seems to serve him well. One is almost afraid of disturbing these fantasy figures created by artist Leza Lidow. (Below) Dining amidst centuries of fantasy embodied in the realism of a seventeenth-century still-life by Heda, fifteenth-century Belgium tapestries, and an eighteenth-century Austrian religious figure blurs the distinction between the real and unreal. The poignant twentieth-century man and woman created by Leza Lidow cannot be easily ignored. Man the builder and destroyer has had large portions of his body removed during the battles he has raged. The woman in the foreground is forever condemned to be an observer through the multitude of windows that pierce her body. She beckons us to discover her real identity by looking into the window openings. (Photos: Toshi Yoshimi)

should clarify why so many Ferraris are bright red), while the Cadillac, Mercedes-Benz, and other more traditionally designed cars symbolize the stability that comes with social acceptance, money, and success.

If you work overtime this week you should rank success and recognition very high on your fantasy list.

More than ten casual sexual encounters this year places you in the same league with professional sexual conquistadores.

When your aphrodisiacs include primarily food and drink that indicates that your social activities may be directed toward prestige or career activities, that is, power. Personal aphrodisiacs such as clothing and fragrances could place your fantasy source somewhere between power and sexual conquest. Aphrodisiacs based on such group indoor sports as hot tubing would definitely be the basis for sexual conquest fantasies.

Masculine and feminine fantasies

Men and women have been socially and economically conditioned to use *different means* to accomplish the same ends. Women have been taught to use sex and love to gain power, and men have frequently used power and status to gain sex and love. Though this may gradually change as women assume more responsible positions and begin to accumulate wealth, male and female fantasies still revolve around sex and power.

Female fantasies frequently deal with conquest, but are more subtle in approach. Romantic dreamlike seduction scenarios are acted out in a variety of settings, with water a popular background. Men have fantasized or eroticized women as mermaids, and there has always been an exotic link between women and aquatic birds. Numerous legends such as Leda and the Swan indicate that this erotic symbolism has been buried in our common psyche since the stone age. In ancient times the giant swan soaring across the heavens was associated with power; gliding across water, it became a fertility symbol. This, combined with the belief that the souls of young virgins slept in the bosom of the swan, gave the birds a magical, if not sacred, significance.

(Top) Modern-day virgins can still slumber in the breast of an etched acrylic swan designed by Jerry Barich. (Source: Versailles Collection)

(Above) Men have always fantasized about women in relation to aquatic birds. The ancient belief that the souls of young virgins slept in the breasts of swans may have been the basis for the design of the bed in this 1925 Theda Bara movie. (Photo: Bettman Archives)

A 1925 movie, "The Golden Bed," captures this fantasy as Theda Bara slumbers in the bosom of the swan. A magnificent contemporary swan bed proves it is still possible to indulge in this fantasy. The designer of this bed, though not acquainted with the virgin legend, clearly envisioned it as a feminine piece of furniture. But contrary to first impressions, this bed does not fulfill an exclusively feminine fantasy. When the $35,000 bed was displayed many men expressed an irresistible desire to purchase it, not for everyday use, but for a secret love nest. This highly eroticized object, like the diamond, establishes a classic motive for conquest in both men and women.

Norma Talmadge in a scene from an early film called "Deception" illustrates another popular fantasy that is linked to dreams of unlimited wealth and beauty. Traditionally American men have been encouraged to consider "their home their castle," and every woman dreamed of being "treated like a queen" and "placed on a pedestal" by her man.

Theda Bara, this time in "Cleopatra," epitomizes the vamp or the classic female version of the Don Juan fantasy. Mustering all her apparent innocence, she has rendered Caesar helpless and her desire for power and control seems assured. Could that mean that even though many women are deeply involved in their careers, the seductress fantasy lurks within the folds of every black negligee?

Male fantasies consistently deal with power gained through money and sexual conquests. The popularity of the *harem* and the *big-game hunter* fantasy implies that multiple sexual conquests are far better than a singular liaison. Phyllis Morris, a Beverly Hills designer, described a harem fantasy that she fulfilled for a client. He wished to have a newly purchased mansion transformed into a maze of twenty-nine bedroom

(Above left) If the average American man envisions his home as a castle, then surely his wife must be a queen who dwells in luxury. Dreams of royalty are shared by both men and women. (Photo: Bison Archives) (Left) Theda Bara illustrates the importance of the casual expression, the carelessly draped covers, and the proper attire for an important seduction scene. (Photos: Bison Archives)

apartments and one very large dining room. The owner controlled entry into the bedroom apartments by an electronic panel located near his bed. The twenty-nine women who occupied the bedrooms never saw one another except in the evening when they all dined together in the huge dining room.

The harem fantasy appeared repeatedly in early silent films. The interior settings almost always included the use of many floor pillows, large feather fans, and heavily draped ceilings. Regardless of shifting styles or changing tastes, thousands of American restaurant owners rely on this universal harem fantasy as a decorative theme.

The big game hunter fantasy is evident in many interior spaces. In the photograph of Gary Cooper's 1930 den the abundance of hunting trophies clearly indicated a very strong, virile man lived there. Although females hunt for a mate, one rarely observes such an obvious display of her trophies, although the female display of diamond rings does proclaim her conquest. This fantasy, however, becomes a Catch 22. One is never sure who conquered whom.

Are fantasy spaces for everyday use?

Many of the fantasy spaces shown in the remainder of this chapter are not full-time permanent residences, but guest houses, second homes, and private hideaways. They qualify as effective fantasy spaces because they can be revisited from time to time. Erotic fantasy spaces can be enjoyed as settings for parties or for the intimate pleasure of two lovers. They can also serve as a private place when you want to be alone. Regardless of how the following environments are used, you will be able to recognize the ever-popular fantasies subtly blended into the ambience of the space.

(Above right) The harem fantasy is the all-time favorite of both men and women. An early movie depicts the essential furnishings for this setting. (Right) Gary Cooper's early Hollywood home projects an unmistakable image of the masculine big-game hunter. (Photos: Bison Archives)

Lounging in your favorite fantasy

Designer Joszi Meskan was challenged by the request to transform a seldom-frequented bar and lounge into a dazzling, exciting place where people would want to linger. A sensory engineer who obviously understands the importance that fantasy plays in such design, she carefully engineered the space to encourage interaction. The excitement is not provided by blinking lights or by loud music, but by channeling human conversation and a gentle touch of déjà vu, reminding one that this setting bears a strong resemblance to an old persistent fantasy. This is not a bar for cruising, nor for those who are afraid to form relationships.

Achieving this effect entailed bringing many seemingly diverse elements together. The Persian, Mesopotamian, Chinese, and Indian decorative elements found on both the furniture and the accessories all have animals as part of their design. Note the cobra table, the dragon on the pillow, the mythical animal on the table base, and the numerous monkeys used throughout. The curved glass etched with flowing lines and the flowers on some chairbacks are actually Oriental in origin and therefore add to the sense of fantasy.

A predominantly red theme set by the Oriental carpet motif ties the entire lounge together. Black is used to give mystery and depth to the spaces. The loose manner in which the furniture is arranged allows groups to be enlarged or reduced as desired. The upholstery textures and forms are soft, voluptuous, and yielding to the touch.

The lighting plays an important part in creating the balance between the required tension and relaxation that make the space function. The needed contrast and drama are supplied by the down lighting, while a gentle ambience is created by the lamps directing light toward the ceiling. Table lamps complete the sense of residential light. This is very carefully engineered to encourage lingering over drinks.

(Left) The stairway beckons you to enter this intriguing fantasy lounge, Compass Rose, created by designer Joszi Meskan. (Top) Ancient Oriental dragons and monkeys are seen throughout the space on pillows and table bases. The textural contrast between the smooth glossy silks and the yielding furlike velvets enhances the romantic fantasy. (Above) A view from the piano reveals the immensity of the space and the soaring height. Large classic columns are lighted by torcheres. Lighting designer David Winfield Wilson also used residential-type floor lamps to create a soft residential ambience. (Opposite page) An abundance of animal symbolism is found in the fantasy settings. The erect phallic-shaped cobra table placed next to a voluptuously inviting lounge is an example of expert sensory engineering. (Photos: Charles S. White)

A tropical hideaway

This mysterious oasis deep in the tropical jungle beckons us to enter. Large tropical birds, sensing our intrusion, move from branch to branch. Long-handled fans, no longer needed in the chill of the evening, are placed above the mantle. The animal skins covering some of the chairs and the sleek black floor create a tantalizing contrast with the virginal white ruffled cushions. The pairs of pristine chairs pushed close together easily provide seating for two.

This exotic setting, reminiscent of a Rousseau painting, is a romantic illusion created to provide pleasure. A master of the exotic, designer Edward Turrentine proves that actual plants need not be used to create a tropical feeling. The banana trees are painted on the walls, and the birds are frozen in flight by outstanding regional artists.

An occasional lover or overnight guest can be made comfortable on bedding that folds out from the mirrored door armoire. A small shower bath adjoins the area. When the space is being used for a dinner dance or small luncheon, a portable bar and other party equipment can be easily brought into the space.

(Above) This secluded guest house transports you to a lovers' afternoon hideaway in a tropical rain forest where rare birds fly in and out of banana trees.

(Above) This fantasy world, like the lovers who occupy the space, knows no season and will live forever amidst the trompe l'oeil banana trees.

(Opposite page) Virginal white chairs are easily spread apart for use before a cozy fire in the late afternoon. (Photos: Charles S. White)

Disco for a pharaoh

Some have described the work of Phyllis Morris as outrageous. Indeed, it is often shocking since she specializes in fantasy fulfillment for the very wealthy. Hollywood celebrities are quite uninhibited about their fantasies and frequently want to share them with their friends. Producer Allan Carr traveled to Egypt and returned with ideas for several parties. His mansion had always been the site of opulent gatherings, but when he contacted Phyllis Morris about his idea for a disco, it was decided to make it a permanent party area in the basement. Previously it had served as a rehearsal room for such stars as Petula Clark and Ann-Margaret.

The entire design process took about nine months and over $1 million to complete. Mirrors were used to expand what was actually a very small space. Placed on the ceiling and side walls, the mirrors serve to reflect the

newly installed copper floor.

Lighting strips that pulsate to the sound of hard rock music are embedded in the floor and along the edges of the ceiling. The music control system and disk jockey areas can be seen through a round opening in a wall to the rear of a raised platform. This platform is filled with pillows and lounging couches covered in metallic fabrics. Bronze name plates assure Carr's special friends a prominent spot on the platform. (His friends extend the same courtesy to him in their private clubs.)

Heavy bronze doors shaped in the form of the Egyptian sun god open into a small stand-up bar, which is fashioned after Egyptian architectural columns. Glasses and other equipment on the wall behind the bar become lost in the total glitter. Bronzed palm leaves line the ceiling and reinforce the desert fantasy theme Morris created so superbly.

(Right) Dance away the evening in a disco setting fit for a pharaoh. Honored guests dressed in flowing kaftans survey the action from their reserved places on the raised platform of Alan Carr's private fantasy world created by designer Phyllis Morris. (Above) One enters this fantasy world through a door symbolically shaped like the sun. A stand-up bar resembling a stone entry stands before a mirrored liquor cabinet. The copper mirrored ceilings and walls reflect gold and silver palm trees. (Photos: Sheldon Lettich)

Exotic Chinese bedroom

The lure of the Orient is the basis of many fantasies. It sets the entire mood of this bedroom. The designer, Douglas Pierce Hiatt, used twenty-seven variations of mauve and peach to create this warm and cozy feeling. The huge eighteenth-century opium bed dominates this 20-by-25-foot bedroom. The warm romantic pink draws you into the space to explore the delicate carving across the top of the bed. The handpainted fabric used on the bed is tied at the four corners with intricate Oriental knots, and the round pillows have knotted rope tassels. A nineteenth-century Chinese headrest, or neck pillow, is used as a step stool to get into this highrise bed. On the right side of the room an inviting fireplace casts an additional warm glow. To the right of the bed a French-style table holds greenery in antique porcelain Chinese vases painted with wedding scenes.

(Left) Exotic Oriental wedding vases and lush tropical plants set the mood for this Chinese bedroom designed by Douglas Pierce Hiatt. (Below) An antique eighteenth-century Chinese opium bed dominates this warm cozy bedroom. (Photos: Charles S. White)

A lovers' grotto retreat

A married couple with small children commissioned the team of Susanne Dahl and Jerry Barich to design a lovers' grotto—a place where they could escape the everyday pressures that take the romance out of being married. It had to be a separate, almost secret place, set aside only for them.

The hideaway by the sea was selected because they wanted the relaxing atmosphere of the ocean, but they also wanted the elegance afforded by a penthouse. The clients in addition wanted a natural aggregate material, which they produced, to be used throughout the interior.

With this in mind the designers proceded to construct a grotto by the sea. The aggregate stones collected from the beach at La Paz, Mexico, were the chosen surfaces. They were hand set one by one, which interestingly is not any more time consuming than the brick-laying process. Different sizes and colors were used throughout. Stones the size of seeds were laid for the living and dining areas floors, while larger stones were used in the spa area. Because the designers were able to have complete control of the surface, they decided to round all corners, and where walls joined floors the two planes were curved to flow into each other. In addition, wherever possible all doors were removed and openings were given a round shape to increase the organic flowing feeling.

Mirrors were used on the ceilings to expand the space vertically, and the living room ceiling brings the beach into the interior space. The spa provided an ideal setting in which to savor the sensuous delights of unhurried bathing.

The bedroom was carpeted for increased sensuality and the bed designed with a strip of concealed lighting to create a mysterious floating effect. The use of the animal head and the fur rug combined with erotic sculpture from India expressed some significant fantasies.

The environment offers endless contrasts between soft and hard, cold and warm, shinny and dull. It provides the excitement needed to renew romantic, seductive, and sensual delights.

(Opposite page) As one enters this grotto by the sea its unique romantic quality becomes evident. Every surface is covered in pebbles collected from the seaside, with colors ranging from almost black to deep wine. Each stone, individually set, varies from the tiny seed sizes on the floors to large flat sizes on the ceiling. (Left) The dining area is filled with organic forms and symbols. Two walls and the ceiling are mirrored to reflect the glass and stone table and the wooden chairs in natural pale beige tones. (Above) Though built high above the sea, mirrors on the ceiling and numerous glass surfaces bring beach scenes into the living room. The tusk used as a desk base hints at the passionate love that created these spaces. (Photos: Sheldon Lettich)

(Right) Fantasy symbols abound in this bedroom with its dark bronze-mirrored ceiling. The stone used everywhere else on the walls and floor is limited to the bed framing and a half circular area behind the bed. The soft carpeting and the fur on the floor add to the erotic seductive quality. The large animal head over the bed clearly marks this room as male territory. (Below) The bathing grotto contains several stone sizes. The whirlpool bath is elevated on a dais. The mirrors forming an organic curve on one wall reflect the round opening from the bathing grotto into the dining area. Shared eroticism is the object of this fantasy hide-away. (Photos: Sheldon Lettich)

A desert fantasy

The clients gave designer Edward Turrentine only two requirements. They wanted a romantic fantasy space in the shape of a tent and the colors were to be based on the plum-colored nail polish worn by the wife.

To carry out the request, the designer worked with tent weight materials. Regional artists were commissioned to handpaint the canvas in the varying tints and shades of the clients' favorite color. The living room floors were done in a smooth, cool tile. Canvas was also used as an area rug under the sofas. The ceilings were draped with canvas to simulate a tent, and lights were inserted into the folds of the canvas to create a soft glow.

As one moves from room to room one is

A home away from home for married lovers echoes scenes from the Arabian Nights. Designer Edward Turrentine and J. Bevan created a tentlike ceiling and sand-colored floors and walls to complete the fantasy. (Photo: Charles S. White)

aware that the tent atmosphere pervades the space. In a guest room the canvas was stretched at angles across the room and handpainted with palm leaves to simulate an oasis in the desert. The master bedroom is designed like a tent within a tent. The custom-designed master bed with low upholstered ends is placed diagonally on a low platform. Lighted from above and below, the bed seems to float in space. The mosquito netting adds a feeling of mystery.

A subtle Oriental influence is also created by the handpainted consoles in the living room, the handpainted cranes on the den ceiling, and the opium bed used in the guest bedroom.

In place of framed paintings or isolated works of art, Turrentine has made the lighting and the abundant color in the handpainted fabrics provide all the visual stimulus necessary to make the fantasy a reality. Even though canvas is not normally associated with luxury interiors, its abundant use and the manner with which it is draped on the floor convey the essence of opulence.

(Left) A sitting room with partially mirrored walls reflects hand-painted cranes on the ceiling. (Above) The guest bedroom expands the fantasy to include the Orient. (Opposite page) In the master bedroom a custom-built bed is draped with romantic mosquito netting and lit from above and below. (Photos: Charles S. White)

A country estate in Brooklyn

If you went to sleep and awoke in this environment you would think that you had taken a trip through time to the turn of the century. Who is that woman standing on the balcony overlooking the garden? There are birds singing and the sound of wind in the trees, so you must be in the country. From another window you notice a porch overlooking a beach and a lake from which a gentle mist is rising.

Actually you are in a concrete garage without windows in Brooklyn Heights, New York. This is the studio/home of artist, designer, and sensory engineer par excellence Christian Thee.

On closer examination one finds that the lovely lady at the window is actually painted on a panel. The slate floors and even the rich-looking Oriental rug are painted on a wooden surface that has been constructed over the concrete floor.

In the center is a sunken seating area around a fresh-water pond. The skylight above provides light for the plants and flowering shrubs. The entire setting was designed to change from day to night (including the sounds). When night falls one can see an inviting pavilion on the lake. Thee has even arranged so that lights flicker and dancers can be seen moving about in the pavilion.

(Below) When night comes, laughter echoes across the lake and couples can be seen dancing in a mysterious pavilion created by designer Christian Thee. (Opposite page) Fantasies exist at every turn in this Brooklyn Heights windowless concrete garage. On warm evenings, for instance, you may stroll out to the veranda and enjoy the lake vista. (Photos: Jaime Ardiles-Arce)

The bedroom area contains a massive bed, and another cozy seating area. An additional trompe l'oeil painting is seen on the screen near the couch.

The entire environment can be folded away to make room for a working studio in which Thee prepares for painting exhibitions and executes commissions for other designers of interior fantasies.

This is living theater and the most delightful kind of fantasy. The ease with which Christian Thee adapts his excellent background in theater set design and lighting to actual living spaces is remarkable. In the event that our civilization is ever forced to live underground or on orbiting space stations, this particular type of sensory engineering might become a vital link in human adjustment and survival.

(Right) The massive bed is real, so are the records, music system, and seating. The lattice screen on the right is a skillful piece of trompe l'oeil painting. (Opposite page) A beautiful young woman awaits her dinner guests as she surveys a garden below the balcony where birds are singing and wind rustles the trees. If she seems to linger too long at the window, perhaps it is because she is a fantasy created by designer Thee. (Photos: Jaime Ardiles-Arce)

"When did I fall in love, what night, which day?
When did I first begin to feel this way?
How could the moment pass unfelt, ignored?
Where was the blinding flash?
Where was the crashing thud? . . .
When did respect first become affection?
When did affection suddenly soar?"

Sheldon Harnick

Engineering Romantic Settings

The above lyrics from "Fiorello," a 1959 Broadway hit, express the mysterious quality that surrounds everything romantic. The differences that separate romantic, seductive, and sensuous spaces are like the blending of respect, affection, and love. Understanding these subtle relationships holds the key to engineering romantic spaces.

Romantic space evaluator

Erotic energy provides the "blinding flash"; beyond that you must develop the ability to detect the subtle cues, both natural and man-made, that romantic spaces project. The romantic spaces shown throughout Part 2 cover a broad spectrum of romanticism from nature themes to fantasies of faraway times and places. Use the following sets of questions to sharpen your visual awareness of romantic cues.

Apply the questions below to one of the settings in Chapter 3 that impressed you as having the most romantic qualities. From the same chapter evaluate a second space that you did not like quite as well.

An arbor of floral fabrics that can blend with nature can help bring the beauty of springtime into your romantic rooms. (Source: Old West-bury Garden Collection, Brunschwig & Fils, Inc.)

1. Does the space appear to be remote and secluded?

2. Is it reminiscent of a faraway place and time?

3. Does it provoke a feeling of intimacy and coziness?

4. Do the colors and forms appear soft and inviting?

5. Do you want to share the space with someone special?

6. Can the natural lighting be controlled with drapery, blinds, or shutters?

7. Is it located near a lake, river, or ocean?

8. Would the setting provide awesome views of sunsets, the rising moon, an occasional rainbow?

9. Is the artificial lighting soft and low?

10. Are all the elements vital to a romantic space found here (excluding music and fragrances that cannot be shown in a photograph)?

Scoring: Give yourself 10 points for every yes answer. If you scored *10 to 20 points:* Better look elsewhere. This is not the space you would want to share with someone special. If you got *20 to 40 points:* This space would meet some of your romantic needs, but you would not be comfortable here for a long period of time. You would be forced to fre-quently recharge your erotic energy level elsewhere. If you scored between *50 and 100 points:* This could be the setting for your magnificent obsession. It could be a perfect second home or a place you may never want to leave.

Fantasy space evaluator

Chapter 4 provided diverse fantasy settings. This evaluator will help you determine which of them parallels your personal fantasies. If you share your space with someone and have not already compared fantasies, now is the time. Each should evaluate the same space and compare scores later.

1. Does the space provoke a feeling of déjà vu?

2. Does the environment make you feel glamorous, regal, powerful?

3. Does the space make you feel self-conscious about what your friends might say? Afraid they might think you are a bit eccentric?

4. Would you dress to match the mood of the space?

5. Would it be easy to pretend that you were someone else in that space?

6. Does the space provoke a sense of mystery and excitement?

7. When things are not going well, would you find this space a wonderful retreat or fortress against the world?

8. Would your friends be impressed?

9. Does the space make you feel sexy?

10. On first viewing the space, were you overcome with a desire to own it?

Scoring: For each yes answer give yourself 10 points. If you got *10 to 20 points:* You enjoy reading or watching television alone rather than engaging in fantasies with other people. You would probably be embarrassed to live in this space. If you scored between *20 and 40 points:* Your fantasies are usually concerned with finding a means of escape from everyday pressures. A hideaway would answer your needs. If you scored *50 to 100 points:* This space is perfect for you. You have a broad range of fantasies that deal with sex and power. (Is there any other kind?)

Universally romantic

Now that you have determined which of the romantic spaces meet your requirements, you may want to compare your preferences with those that are considered universal. The tree diagram shown on the right (read from top to bottom) illustrates how individual romantic elements relate to each other and contribute to the creation of a romantic atmosphere. This diagram also shows the major part played by the three dominate romantic fantasies:

1. Search for ideal love through a return to nature.

2. Nostalgia or yearning for a faraway time.

3. Escape to exotic faraway places.

These fantasies are revealed to us in the conscious and unconscious ways we fulfill them. For example, a restaurant designed like a tropical jungle fulfills the escape-to-exotic-places fantasy. The disco designed in the style of an Egyptian tomb answers the need for nostalgic fantasy.

When a selected number of romantic spaces from the preceding chapters are evaluated on the basis of universal qualities, it is

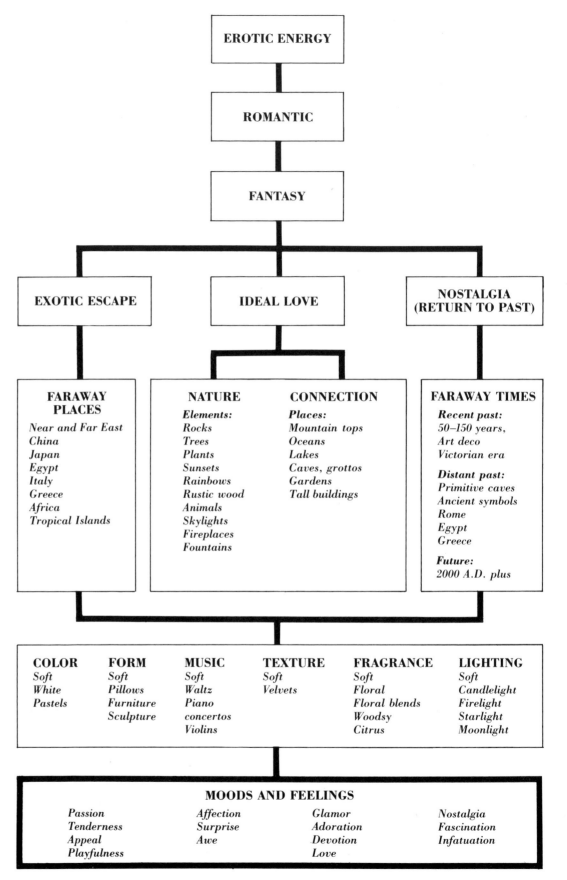

ROMANTIC SETTINGS* Chapters 3 and 4	ROMANTIC ELEMENTS	SEDUCTIVE ELEMENTS	SENSUOUS ELEMENTS
1. Irresistible Beach House	Location: views Colors Fireplace	Mirrors	Spiral stairs
2. Skyline House	Location: views Surfaces: wood Skylights Fireplace		
3. The Coach House	Skylight Plants Nostalgia: art collection		
4. Inspired Echoes	Fireplace Nostalgia: faraway time and place (China) Plants		
5. Penthouse Panorama	Height: view Piano Art	Mirrors	
6. Magnificent Memories	Nostalgia: art deco Fireplace	Vivid colors Glittering fabrics	Furniture forms Sculpture
7. Lounging in Your Favorite Fantasy	Nostalgia: places, time, colors Ancient symbols: snakes	Furniture: lounges	
8. A Country Estate in Brooklyn	Nostalgia: time Plants Water: views		
9. Disco for a Pharaoh	Nostalgia: faraway places	Glittering lights Mirrors	Textures
10. A Lovers' Grotto Retreat	Nostalgia: time/rocks Symbols: animal forms Fireplace Location: view	Mirrors Animal fur Large spa Tusks	Furniture forms
11. A Desert Fantasy	Nostalgia: faraway time, place Colors Animals		
12. Exotic Chinese Bedroom	Nostalgia: faraway places, time (China) Fireplace Plants		

important to note that some of the spaces also contain seductive and sensuous universal cues. When those environments are analyzed as on the accompanying table and bar chart, you can visually distinguish the differences among romantic spaces. For example, the Disco for a Pharaoh (page 60) and A Lovers' Grotto Retreat (pages 62–64) contain certain elements that span all three categories of erotic spaces. Though predominantly romantic in atmosphere, the grotto with its blending of cues from all three areas would prove more interesting over a longer period of time. You can use this same method to evaluate your own spaces or to check out the number of romantic elements in your favorite restaurant.

(Opposite page) The romantic tree diagram shows (read from top to bottom) the various components needed to create a romantic environment. Compare it with the erotic wheel on page 16. (Left) The romantic, seductive, and sensuous elements used to create the romantic settings featured in Chapters 3 and 4 are listed in this table.

*Note: This evaluation is based on the visual elements in the photographs. It does not include factors such as music, fragrance, changes in lighting that could intensify the romantic atmosphere or make it more seductive or sensuous.

ROMANTIC SPACES*	ROMANTIC	SEDUCTIVE	SENSUOUS
Space 1	███████	████	██
Space 2	███████		
Space 3	███████		
Space 4	███████		
Space 5	███████	███	
Space 6	███████	█████	
Space 7	███████	█████	
Space 8	███████		
Space 9	███████	█████	
Space 10	███████	████	██
Space 11	███████		
Space 12	███████		

*Note: Spaces that span one or more categories of erotic spaces will be the most successful in meeting your changing moods. Readers may identify additional elements based on personal preferences.

Furnishings, accessories, and textures

Colors, forms, textures, and lighting become the sum total of everything placed in a space. Many manufactured and custom-made furnishings are available to use in your romantic erotic spaces. Their use, however, does not have to be limited to romantic spaces. All spaces can have romantic overtones.

Beds: Of course, one of the most important items in your romantic environment will be the bed. Some sensory engineers claim that they often begin their entire design plan with the selection of the bed. Therefore it is not surprising to find an abundance of romantic beds. The majority are designed with four tall corner posts that support a full-sized canopy. Although the underside of some canopied beds intended for seduction may be covered with mirrors to serve as an erotic stimulus, a romantic canopied bed would not have mirrors.

Wicker four-poster beds evoke a romantic response. The natural wicker used in combination with sensuous materials seems to create an irresistible appeal. The wicker is associated with the aura of a faraway tropical place, and the use of mosquito netting emphasizes this theme. The unexpected addition of satin bed coverings shown on the top right of page 77 makes this setting provocative. Men, in particular, expressed a strong preference for this bed. Perhaps the size of the corner supports projects a feeling of sturdiness and strength that is found desirable.

Your choice of the whimsical Seguaro cactus bed could create the basis for an exotic fantasy setting. Some more traditional beds are designed with a sense of nostalgia for our own American colonial heritage. The Hermitage bed is an excellent example. The hand-crocheted canopy and thin Sheraton-style posts project a delicately restrained, yet romantically feminine image. The brass bed is appropriately named the Queen's Crown and would make an exuberant romantic Victorian statement in any space.

(Opposite page top) The bar chart shows the range of erotic cues listed in the table on page 75. (Opposite page bottom) Our American heritage is evident in this delicate four-poster bed with a hand-crocheted canopy by Norman of Salisbury.

(Top left) The hand-carved Seguaro bed designed by an Arizona architect is a whimsical bit of interior landscaping. (Source: Martin Klein Designs) (Above) Create a romantic Victorian atmosphere in any bedroom with a brass bed. (Source: Brass Bed Company)

(Top right) The large four poster designed by Edward Li becomes irresistibly sexy with the addition of satin and net. (Source: Innovative Marketing) (Above) The smaller-scaled bed designed by Peter Rocchia for Wicker Works is shown with small printed cotton fabrics that create a romantic country mood.

Tables: The primary purpose of a table is to serve; and its decorative symbolism is always secondary to that. The tables in this section range from those designed to be used beside the bed to those large enough for dining. Those shown on this page are romantic nostalgia and would be ideal in settings designed for magnificent obsessions described in Chapter 4. The Cygnet table, like the others in this group, echoes the ancient symbols that form a large part of our fantasies. The tables shown on page 79 are also designed for fantasy settings. One is covered in snake skin, with the cobra used as a structural element, while the other has a coiling cobra snake form as a support for a glass top.

(Above and right) Tables can also set the mood for a room. Try a hand-carved French Baroque table for a sophisticated look. (Above: source: Edward Pashayan) Country French-style furniture (right) can create an informal effect. (Right: source: IPF International) (Above right) The Cygnet table designed by Cebe makes use of the ancient swan symbol. (Source: Farallon Studio) (Opposite page top left) Clear Plexiglass etched with a circle of elephants would make a big-game hunter feel at home. (Source: Versailles Collection) (Opposite page top right) Brass gazelles known for their lean, beautiful silhouettes are used as a base for this table. (Source: Teakwood, Inc.) (Opposite page bottom left and right) The powerful symbolism of the cobra is used in the design of these two tables. The top of the far right table is covered with snake skins. (Source: Elodia, Inc.)

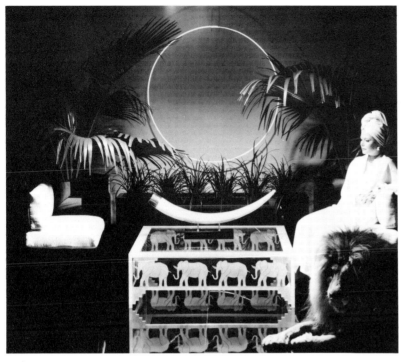

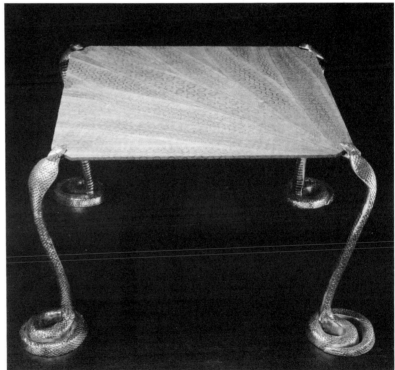

Lamps and accessories: The desire to travel to exotic places can in part be satisfied by surrounding yourself with authentic artifacts from other lands. Fantasies can be sparked, for instance, by a Tibetan dance mask or a Philippine statue of the Rice God.

Lamps can also take on strange fantasy forms. Many are designed in the image of winged animals that may appear in our most private fantasies. The marvelously eroticized ostrich floor lamp shown on the bottom left of this page would be perfect in any harem or Theda Bera fantasy where the quality of lighting would be of no immediate concern.

(Far left) Floor lamp makes use of exotic floral and bird forms that add a sense of mystery to any romantic setting. (Source: Arte Bella, Inc.) (Left) For those special exotic fantasies, the Marc II Gallery imports authentic Tibetan masks and other South Atlantic artifacts. (Bottom left) Fit for a Theda Bara movie, this ostrich feather floor lamp and cobra table would make excellent harem accessories. (Source: Elodia, Inc.) (Below) This custom-designed interpretation of Leda and the Swan is a sculptured glass panel made by Bolae.

Specific textures: Although soft textures usually dominate most romantic settings, that does not limit your choices. For example, the floor may be covered in soft plush carpeting, a beautiful Oriental rug, or perhaps an occasional fur. Whether your space has been designed for nostalgia or pure fantasy, an Oriental rug can transform an ordinary space into a unique setting.

The fabrics used on the furniture, drapery, and walls can vary from rich Indian paisley patterns in silk, wool, or cotton to fabrics that celebrate all the glories of a romantic country flower garden. Flowers can also turn wild and lush like those from a rain forest fantasy in a painting by Rousseau. The examples on pages 81–82 prove that the range can be endlessly exciting.

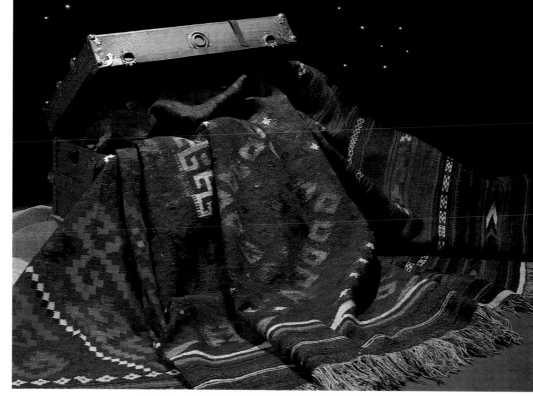

(Clockwise from top) Brightly colored Kilim rugs are excellent for many types of romantic settings. (Source: Merit Carpet Corporation) (Above) Like a backdrop for a Rousseau jungle painting. "South Island" fabric could create a jungle fantasy. (Source: S. Harris and Company) (Left) A beautifully executed paisley in wool, silk, or cotton could be incorporated into many types of romantic fantasies. (Source: Cowtan and Tout) (Above left) Pastel handwoven dhurries from Rosecore are the perfect addition to romantic settings. A rug with classic Chinese symbols enhances a Far Eastern theme. (Source: Indrahma by Rahmanan)

(Clockwise from right) Zebra rugs, whether real or stenciled, can add exciting fantasy details to your spaces. The rustic chairs are from Wicker Works. (Bottom right) This French-style Oriental rug with its pastel colors is traditionally used to create a romantic setting. (Bottom) "Jacquar" is another fabric that could add a little of the wild to your interiors. (Source: Karl Mann Associates) (Below) The fabric on this comforter is tufted in a fish-scale pattern. (Source: Designed by Michael Childers for International Down Shops)

Romantic bath environments: Any bath can be transformed into a romantic delight, for example, by using an exquisite wash basin handpainted with colorful poppies. For the nostalgic bath there are fittings that simulate the age of Wedgewood and candlelight. Or faucets can capture the opulence of royalty or a creation from one of your fantasies.

Three unusually romantic bath accessories were designed by Artistic Brass. The blue Wedgewood faucet set (above) is delicately detailed for use in a period-style bath. A sparkling set of exquisitely cut crystal faucets (above left) and whimsical brass dolphins (left) would make a beautiful addition to any romantic bath.

(Right) A miniature botanical garden is created by Sherle Wagner's organically styled wash basins. (Below) A detail of a wash basin with hand-painted poppies. (Source: Sherle Wagner Exclusive)

PART THREE

SEDUCTIVE INTERIORS

6

Hors d'Oeuvre Environments

Hors d'oeuvre spaces reflect the mounting erotic energy level that accompanies the transition from entry-level romanticism to high-voltage sensuousness. These environments represent a shift of emphasis from idealized love to sexual gratification.

Each person approaches seduction differently, but most seduction scenarios tend to be either subtle or aggressive. The art of subtle seduction has traditionally been considered a feminine trait, reflecting the female emotional and physical makeup that requires a gradual increase in erotic energy. The aggressive masculine seductive approach, on the other hand, expresses the more immediate nature of male sexual response. These major differences, therefore, are reflected in the way spaces are designed.

Western culture has frequently suppressed overt seductive spaces such as public bath houses and bordellos (discussed in Chapter 8). With the advent of the male-oriented Sexual Revolution aggressive seductive spaces were introduced into the public arena as discos and singles bars, which have been influencing personal relationships for the past three decades. This chapter will review both public and private masculine-type seductive spaces.

Don Juan entertaining at an "at-home" happy hour. (Photo: Warner Brothers, 1926; Bison Archives)

Singles bars: big-game hunting territory

Singles bars should not be confused with pubs or friendly neighborhood taverns that traditionally answered men's need to congregate outside their domesticated environments. These public taverns brought men together from all social strata and guaranteed nothing but relaxed fraternal fellowship.

Though the pub is still alive and well, something called the "cocktail party" launched a new social custom in America during the late forties or early fifties. (No one is quite sure about the dates, but it oddly precedes the growing interest in women's equal rights of the sixties.) These cocktail parties drew men and women together for a few hours of social drinking in private homes, thus marking the beginning of "small talk" and a whole new era of more casual relationships.

The pressures of the Sexual Revolution combined with women's quest for equality were largely responsible for transferring the cocktail party to public spaces, which became known as "cocktail lounges." Women, erroneously believing that pubs and taverns had finally been opened to them, flocked to cocktail lounges as a symbol of their liberation. Within the next ten years these lounges evolved into singles bars. Each step in the evolution from the cocktail lounge to the singles bar increased a reliance on the bar environment as a magic showcase for sexual magnetism.

Men and women singles, long considered decadent and a threat to society, were transformed into worldly playboys and playgirls. The big-game hunt with sexual favors as trophies created ruthless competition in singles bars. There was pressure to "score," to find someone to take home for the evening; there was also pressure to invent another clever way of saying, "Your place or mine?" Going from bar to bar, or cruising, until one found a place with the right male/female mix or the general ambience that suited your mood could be very time consuming. As bars increased in numbers, a bar subculture developed its own set of social rules. *Esquire* recently published a *Guide to the 100 Best Bars in America.* After a careful survey they classified them according to the poshest, the most inexpensive, most laid-back (relaxed), most swinging, and most honky-tonk.

"How-to" books offering advice on establishing intimacy with others in less than five minutes became very popular. Learning to score without having to spend too much time or money on drinks was elevated to an art. It was believed that if one actually sat down with someone at a table, it would in some way imply a form of commitment. Therefore, to speed up the process of selecting a sexual mate for the evening, small stand-up bars, or standing tables, were distributed about the area. This made it possible to cruise the bar, make eye contact, and perhaps exchange a few words without getting emotionally involved.

Late in the 1970s sensitive men and women began to resent the dehumanizing effects of these obvious sexual swap-meets. Sensing the changing attitudes, bar owners tried many new devices to continually lure people, particularly women, into their bars. "Happy hours" (actually revivals of the late-afternoon cocktail party) and special "ladies days" made drinks available at half price. Some bars even raffled off romantic vacations with eligible bachelors as a lure. One bar owner commented, "The bar that attracts the most women will be the most successful."

Designer of these hors d'oeuvre environments also sought to subdue their overt purpose by designing pseudo-romantic spaces that ranged from mildly to highly nostalgic. For instance, entire interiors of old English pubs were transported to America piece by piece to further the romantic illusion. Some bars have a country store look; others project a more sophisticated art deco look of the twenties.

But even with these changes a certain segment of the single population will never return. They are instead gravitating toward health-pub clubs. To avert this trend bars may someday install health exercise equipment and establish smoking and nonsmoking areas.

Discotheques: settings for instant seduction

Though not an American innovation the discotheque was to become the ultimate setting spawned by the Sexual Revolution. Designed as nontouching spaces, the disco's incessant flickering and flashing lights combined with mirrors and highly erotic music forced aggressive seductive tensions to mount. All contact was visually oriented; even small talk was impossible. The sense of the unexpected and the nonpermanence of life, coupled with this rapidly changing spatial atmosphere, caused people to act out their seductive fantasies in the sparkling, revealing evening clothes they wore and the way they danced.

(Opposite page) The Bonds Disco is a fantasy land of pulsating colors designed by Shelton Stortz and Mendel. (Above left) Observe the dancing at Bonds Disco from an area inhabited by red-hot aquatic creatures. (Left) Time out from dancing at the Bonds Disco to share encounters with strange silver animals. (Photos: Bo Parker) (Above) Disco surfaces expand in every direction and purposely create visual disorientation. (Photo: NeoRay)

Many disco interiors ran the gamut from hard-edged futuristic to bizarre dreamlike themes.

The Bonds Disco in New York City designed by Shelton Stortz and Mendel, for instance, had dreamlike furnishings in areas adjacent to the dance floor. In one seating area huge silver cows could be seen lounging about, and in another spot overlooking the dance floor patrons might stumble upon glowing red spiny underwater creatures while a huge red octopus form undulates above.

At-home discos became a popular form of West Coast entertainment. Many wealthy people preferred to boogie in the privacy of their own homes because it provided an opportunity to impress their friends with their creative use of space, and it also was a perfect excuse to indulge their personal fantasies. The home disco could range from an all-out fantasy like the Egyptian tomb of Allan Carr in Chapter 3 to the high-technology space-age look of the private disco designed by Charles Burke. This disco had a huge control room overlooking the 20-by-25-foot dancing space dominated by a large light sculpture that pulsates to the music. To further enhance the fantasy ambience, guests were frequently surrounded by clouds of mist created by dry ice.

(Below left) It is possible to play out your private fantasies in your own disco; this one was designed by Charles Burke. (Below) At private disco parties guests dance below a pulsating custom-designed light sculpture. (Opposite page) Note the space-ship-type control center for a private home disco. (Photos: Toshi Yoshimi)

A romantic disco fantasy

Although The Oz Disco was completed at the peak of disco popularity in 1980, Joszi Meskan consciously or unconsciously designed a schizophrenic space that clearly forecasts the romantic revival of the eighties. The large 5000-square-foot space on the 32nd floor of the Hotel St. Francis in San Francisco is divided into two distinct floor levels. The entry level leads to the disco dance floor, the main service bar, and numerous stand-up bars. As patrons approach the disco dancing area they walk past rows of tall vertical mirrors, rock formations, and trees. On reaching the rocks and the stair guests are assigned numbered seating on either the upper or lower levels.

Strolling through both the raised and lowered spaces, one immediately notices that the lower area contains many cozy romantic nooks and quiet corners where lovers might watch the twinkling lights of San Francisco. The mirrors flanking the windows reflect both the disco lights and the lights of the city below. The abundance of trees, chairs constructed of rustic twigs, natural rocks, and ferns add to the romantic atmosphere. Many guests prefer seating in the upper disco dancing area because they want to be a part of the action. Obviously the Oz is still dominated by a disco image. But as discomania boggies into the sunset, the Oz has only to expand its romantic area and add soft music for its transformation to be complete.

(Above) A wooded disco atop the Hotel St. Francis in San Francisco was designed by Joszi Meskan. (Right) Combining pulsating disco lights and sounds with this idyllic romantic setting creates a strange contrast. (Opposite page) Find a romantic spot for watching the San Francisco Bay. (Photos: Jaime Ardiles-Arce)

Masculine personal seductive spaces

In a 1926-film based on the adventures and sexual conquests of Don Juan, John Barrymore conducted most of his seductions in the privacy of his home. It contained a large circular room that featured what was probably the first American "conversation pit." The scene shown on page 86 has the playboy bachelor hosting an at-home happy hour (customary before the advent of singles bars). Careful scrutiny of this setting reveals all the items that later became standard equipment in the American bachelor pad. Notice the design and location of the furnishings. The large round sectional seating assured that everyone could become friendly, and the huge table in the center could also be used for becoming more intimate. Even the wedge-shaped back cushions of the sofa were designed for lounging. This seating may have served as the prototype for the many pieces of erotic furniture designed since the sixties.

In addition to furnishings, many ingenious new uses of space were devised to lure the seductee into bed or the pit. Those who love romantic nostalgia may want to consider the advantages of the old-fashioned swing. Swings have a long history and have often been used to add that touch of erotic playfulness so necessary in all good seduction scenarios. The one on page 95 illustrates a "swing-in" conversation pit designed for a winter ski lodge hideaway.

In some bachelor dwellings the pit may even resemble an animal lair. The designer of an old movie set produced the epitome of the romantic seductive den. It belonged to a big strong game hunter with a primitive approach. How else could he have acquired all the skins?

The bachelor pad: success or failure?

If the success of an environment can be measured by the length of time it lingers in the memory of one who experiences it, then the bachelor pad must be declared a masterful design concept. Remembering her first encounter with a bachelor pad over twelve years before, a New York woman was able to give a detailed description, of not only the furnishings, but the mood of the space and her reactions.

The colors, textures, and furnishings are listed in the order she remembered them:

1. Red everywhere.
2. Mirrors on the walls and over the bed.
3. Fake fur.
4. Large bed, filled with water.
5. Bean bag chair and pillows.
6. Music throughout.

Her emotional reactions to the space remained equally vivid: an instant feeling of being trapped, followed by the overwhelming urge to turn and flee. She felt "repulsion" at what she described as an "overkill" not unlike that of a used-car salesman trying to score on a weekly tally sheet.

Women all over America can probably match this description word for word. How could so many bachelors have turned off so many women?

The answer lies in an examination of the goals and purposes of the bachelor pad. Male-envisioned and male-designed, the bachelor pad was supposed to guarantee successful sexual conquests. One bachelor confided to his designer: "I want the women I bring here to immediately be reduced to a moist quivering state of arousal." This request clearly shows that these spaces were meant to serve as replacements for foreplay. That the space was a turn-on for men and a turn-off for women lies in the fact that men and women respond to seduction differently. That bachelor pads leave no question in anyone's mind about what is to happen there perhaps explains why this approach misses the mark. The next chapter will show examples of successfully blended male and female spaces.

(Opposite page left) Big-game hunters of the sixties enjoyed the conversational challenges provided by the "Safari" modular seating designed by Stendig. (Opposite page above) Contemporary conversation pits still make excellent places for happy-hour talk. (Photo: Thayer Coggins) (Opposite page below) Some bachelors prefer a furry den with overtones of animal lust and conquest. (Photo: Fox Studios, 1920; Bison Archives) (Above) A swing-in playpen provides a popular setting for lovers to pass the time. (Photo: Bo Parker)

Seductive Settings for Busy Singles

New York Times article late in 1982 discussed "sex stereotypes" in the design of space.[1] This seems plausible considering cultural traditions: Little girls' rooms are usually designed with lace and ruffles, while little boys' rooms are designed like space ships. And lest we forget these childhood traditions, taste-makers, aided and abetted by manufacturers, constantly remind us that there are proper settings for each sex.

In 1929 when Emily Post wrote about an appropriate house or room for a man she was merely echoing what had become well-established tradition. She warned housewives that every normal man would and should be repelled by any suggestion of "effeminacy" in his private room or study. She advised the use of wood-panelled walls, sturdy tables, and a comfortable chair upholstered in leather or dark-colored velveteen. In short, she felt that all rooms of "dignity and untrimmed simplicity" were suitable for a man. The most important thing any homemaker could provide a man was the "assurance of unsoilability" because no man could spend his time worrying about a few ashes on the carpet or a stain on the upholstery.[2]

All the books and articles written about how to properly decorate a space for the "man of the house" were based exclusively on the known characteristics of the domesticated male. We were well into the Sexual Revolution before anyone considered that the spatial needs of the single man might be quite different from those of the domesticated male. The emergence of totally masculine spaces in the form of bachelor pads provided some valuable insights. Recent psychological research indicates that "the concept of toughness," or masculine (macho) behavior, is almost entirely something that concerns men in relation to *other men* rather than in relation to women.[3] Therefore it is easy to understand why not only his personal space, but everything owned by the predominantly success-oriented single man, must project a power image to other men. In the last few years books have been written on "power decorating" for the single man, and there is now a firm in Dallas, Texas, that specializes in interior design for single men who want to project the success image to their business associates. Maybe that is an update on the old saying that "every man's home is his castle."

The analysis of bachelor pads in Chapter 6

highlighted how the sexual differences between men and women produced different spatial needs. It is also interesting to observe how men and women differ in their approach to solving spatial needs. Men tend to seek the services of designers and take an active role in the final selections and decisions about the space. They never seem concerned about the possibility of sharing this space with a future partner or whether the space could accommodate two people.

The single woman, on the other hand, does not frequently enlist the services of a professional designer. Some designers think this may be the result of traditional attitudes that women have an innate talent for decorating their homes. Besides, the American woman has been well trained in the fine art of cloning interiors by numerous home decorating magazines. Other designers acknowledge that single women are often not in a financial position to afford the services of a professional. But regardless of financial circumstances, the single woman usually spends less money than a single man on designing her personal space. Audio equipment, a completely stocked bar, imported furnishings, and exercise equipment are some of the more expensive items men consider a must.

However, the most important observation made by designers about single women, regardless of age or social and financial status, was their concern about pleasing the man who may currently share their spaces or some future man who may become a part of

---

[1] Joseph Giovannini, "Sex Stereotypes in Design," *The New York Times*, Dec. 16, 1982.

[2] Emily Post, *The Personality of the House*, New York: Funk and Wagnalls, 1930.

[3] Dick Pothier, "Cultural Rules Inhibit Emotions in Men," *Phoenix Republic* (Knight Rider), September 1982.

Garnet-colored satin from floor to ceiling was combined with art deco furniture by designer Dennis Abbé to create this seductive setting. (Photo: Ambrose Cucinotta)

their lives. One designer concluded that women tend to be very "considerate and sensitive" to masculine psychological spatial needs. Women consciously or unconsciously consider their single quarters a temporary stopover on the way to making a permanent home. Is it cultural conditioning, or perhaps nature's effort to preserve the species through some form of prenatal psychic programming, that causes women to spend their single life on hold?

Can a chrome-and-glass person ever find lasting happiness with a ruffles-and-lace person?

When lovers decide to make a commitment, who, what, which preference prevails? In a 1954 how-to on decorating the "master" bedroom, the author stated that many men left all the decisions to their wives, trusting that they would show some "consideration of his masculinity." Women were cautioned to give up their pink taffeta vanity tables and be ready to compromise, or they might face the divorce courts.

When designers of very posh bachelor penthouses were asked how their clients coped with the bedroom decor after finding a partner, they admitted that compromises must still be made. They preferred to call it a "blending of lifestyles." They found that in cases where spatial preferences could not blend, the dominant partner usually dictated the decor or the relationship would begin to weaken. On the other hand, they found that after marriage many men shifted their energies to career concerns and appeared relieved at not being faced with design decisions. No longer having to display that macho bachelor image to his friends, married men often seemed content to become the domesticated men described by Emily Post.

Though a volatile and ambiguous subject, that of masculine and feminine space should be given more in-depth research for use by designers of residential and commercial spaces. To gain a preliminary understanding of spatial preferences, as well as responses to universal cues, the author used a visual descriptive survey to elicit spontaneous reactions. The eight bedrooms shown on pages 100–101 were used to trigger instant responses. Before proceding, you might like to check your responses to the rooms:

— Bedroom you find the most romantic?

— Personal choice for own bedroom?

— The most sexy room?

— The most feminine room?

— The most masculine room?

These rooms were shown to about 100 people, both males and females whose educational backgrounds ranged from high school to college graduate and whose ages ranged from 19 to 65.

The room selections are listed according to frequency of choice:

1. The most romantic bedroom:

   Room 1

   Room 5

   Room 3

   Room 2

2. Personal choice for own bedroom:

   Room 1

   Room 3

   Room 7

3. The most sexy room:

   Room 5

   Room 1

   Room 6

4. The most feminine room:

   Room 5

   Room 2

   Room 3

5. The most masculine room:

   Room 6

   Room 8

The majority of women selected room 1 as romantic. Men predominantly selected the silver, satin all-white room (5) as being both romantic and sexy. It was surprising to find that the majority of both men and women of all ages selected the same white, silver room (5) as the most feminine, closely followed by the large draped bed (2). The room with many plants was a third choice (3). Despite the lacy "feminine" table and chairs, many men were drawn to this room because of the plants. Both men and women selected the room with the large tapestry on the wall (6) as an example of a very masculine room. Many women also considered this room sexy. The all-brown room with the fur throw on the bed (8) was also considered very masculine.

These rooms represent a wide range of colors, textures, and shapes. The yellow bedroom (4) was not chosen in any category. Many commented favorably on the room and its contents, but it was not selected as having erotic qualities. If you check the color value scale shown in Chapter 2, you will see that yellow is the only color on the scale that does not extend beyond three. Its lack of value ranges probably accounts for the responses.

Most totally white rooms have a tendency to intimidate people. Both men and women fear that they will violate the pure virginal space. Yet the silver and satin white room (5) was very popular. This can be explained by the fact that the silver shiny surface projects very seductive sensuous cues. An all-white room in different textures that do not shine (shown on page 99) provoked such feelings as "cold, prissy, sterile, aloof, pure," and observers thought that the space was appropriate for a "virginal young lady." This verifies a well-known fact about the effect of textures on colors.

Conclusions. This survey pointed out an almost unanimous agreement between men and women on the most romantic, most sexy, most feminine, and most masculine rooms. This indicates that American men and women respond to the same universal cues that symbolize "romantic, sexy, feminine, and masculine," but if the cues become too obvious or highly charged with erotic energy, we do not choose to live in them on a daily basis. This may explain why the room considered the most romantic (1) was also the room selected by both sexes as their personal choice.

(Left) A pristine white room. (Photo: Katzenbach & Warren)

(Overleaf) Bedroom settings 1 through 8 were used as part of a survey to determine attitudes to the colors and moods of highly eroticized bedrooms. [Designers: (1) James Blakeley III; (2) Joyce Colter and Ron Hines; (3) Ron Fields; (4) Steven Chase; (5) Bill Hamilton; (6) Bob Mitchell; (7) Charlotte Finn; (8) Michael Vincent.] (Photographer for rooms 1–6 and 8: Leeland Lee. Photo room 7: Tom Yee)

1

2

3

4

5

6

7

8

SEDUCTIVE SETTINGS FOR BUSY SINGLES

Seductive spaces designed for single men

Some claim that the living spaces of men and women take on different qualities. Many women claim they can sense when a man's apartment has been shared by a female partner. They say it is not a question of finding some makeup or clothing lying about. It is usually something very subtle—perhaps the arrangement of a chair, the way dishes are stacked in the cupboards, or the type of towels in the linen closet. What is this difference? Can men also sense whether a man has previously occupied a space?

The following examples of apartments for single men were all designed by professional designers. Other than one space that was shared by partners, all men lived alone at the time the spaces were designed. What are some subtle differences between these spaces and those designed for women later in this chapter?

(Right) In a bachelor apartment designed for two by Phyllis Morris this satin upholstered bed was meant to be caressed. (Opposite page) Glittering bars are essential to some seductive spaces. (Overleaf) Romantic plants enhance this seductive living room. (Photos: Sheldon Lettich)

Some things speak for themselves

Design on this apartment began while the bachelor shared the space with a partner, so designer Phyllis Morris was challenged to skillfully blend masculine and feminine preferences.

The living room makes use of mirrors to expand the space and add glitter to the general atmosphere. The sparkling city lights combined with the fireplace and plants add the necessary romantic elements. The lines of the sofa and the satin pillows make a beautiful combination of seductive sensuality. On the other side of the living room a very seductive bar is surrounded by banana plants, some painted and others etched on the bar mirrors. The touches of black add a sense of mystery to this seductive room.

The bedroom is oozing with feminine sensuality and seductiveness. The heavily upholstered bed is a tactile delight that begs to have every inch of its taut smooth curves caressed. Other tactile pleasures tempt you at every turn in this room. Portions of the walls are also upholstered in white satin and mirrors cover the ceiling, side walls, and portions of the wall behind the bed.

This home is indeed an excellent example of an environment that can adapt to the romantic, seductive, or sensuous moods of either a man or a woman.

Mood-altering space

Owning several homes in different parts of the world makes it possible for this bachelor to reserve at least one of them as a personal hideaway. This condominium was designed as a creative refuge for a composer of music. Vast interior spaces soaring four stories reverberate with the psychic energy of newly composed music.

Because the owner requested a mood-altering space, designer David James purposely took a sensuous approach. The interior was stripped bare of all unnecessary decor to allow the space to fully respond to a variety of mood changes. During the day there is no attempt to distract from the commanding view of the sea and the changing light as the sun moves across the sky. In the evening the romantic ebb and flow of the sea and brillance of the sun give way to highly charged seductive spaces. Do the composer's creative energies rise in the evenings to match the energy of the space?

The theatrical lighting combined with the high-tech seating/scaffolding seems very appropriate for this large open space. During the evening hours lighting levels can be lowered or raised to change the moods of the space. Magenta-colored jells were selected for most of the lights because the color compliments skin tones.

Living and sleeping quarters on the third and fourth floors provide a peaceful retreat from the seductive open area. Time can be spent in reverie on a third-floor balcony overlooking the sea.

(Top) A stage set for some magnificent seduction scenario by designer David James. (Right) Inspirational spaces were specially designed for a composer of music. (Photos: David Glomb)

Provocative seduction

Platforms throughout this small apartment create an unusual sense of seduction. The provocative rise and fall of space levels that obscure some areas from view while allowing others to playfully coax you to enter are, in some respects, similar to the concept of an animal's lair.

Rather than having traditional seating in this apartment, the entire living environment is one vast lounging area. Designer Tom Foerderer covered all the areas in a low-level loop carpet and designed large comfortable black pillows as back supports to be used wherever lounging occurs. The dining area is located on the ground floor but is also an integral part of the entire living room structure. The black-lacquered table and banquette seating are highlighted by colored neon tubing that visually separates this space from the rest of the area. From a ledge above the dining area large phallic-shaped ceramic pieces dominate the entire living room. A black cantilever structure conceals the lighting as well as electronic sound equipment.

The same platform shapes are repeated in the bedroom. Storage and lighting are concealed in a black-lacquered cantilever unit similar to the one used in the living room. The bed is built into a raised platform and is angled to take advantage of the view. Another black sculptured storage unit houses the television at the foot of the bed. Though designed for a bachelor, this space is now shared by partners.

*(Opposite page left)
Designer Tom
Foerferer angled bed
to allow views from the
window or the enter-
tainment center. (Op-
posite page top right)
Foerferer carefully de-
signed cantilever black
sculptural elements to
house lighting and
storage throughout the
apartment. (Opposite
page bottom right)
Spaces half hidden
from view become very
provocative. (Left)
Masculine erotic space
is dominated by phal-
lic-shaped ceramic
sculpture. (Photos:
Mark Ross)*

Dazzling seduction

Richard Ohrbach and Lynn Jacobson have designed living spaces for Liza Minnelli, the Duke and Duchess of Windsor, Hubert Givenchy, Henry Fonda, Neil Sedaka, among many other celebrities. Designer Ohrbach's own living environment can best be described as mysterious, glamorous, and seductive. On entering his apartment one is unprepared for the sensory experiences encountered there. Surrounded by almost total darkness, black mirrors, subtle fragrances, and vivid islands of color, you are seductively drawn deeper into the space. Although the colored light sources are visible, they are not pulsating lights that hamper your ability to focus. Instead they force your attention on a few intensely colored stationary objects. A vase of red flowers, fire red crystal balls, and brilliantly colored pillows become visual anchors in this seemingly endless space. The lights of Lincoln Center below and the buildings of lower Manhattan in the distance provide additional glitter on walls and ceilings.

Though the apartment is tiny, the darkness creates a conceptual space that transcends actual space limitations, as guests lounge on pillows stacked around a low table or on the leather-covered lounging bed. When guests gather for such special occasions as the Academy Awards, they can watch the elegant affair on two television screens. On more intimate occasions when a low table is set for dining and the chrome vertical blinds are closed, the space becomes a world set apart from reality.

(Below left) Hypnotic colors and shapes force a response to this mysterious and seductive environment designed by Richard Ohrbach. (Below) Dining becomes a color-filled experience. (Opposite page) The city lights extend this seemingly endless space into infinity. (Photos: Mark Ross)

Seductive settings for women

Nostalgia is frequently used in seductive settings designed for women because it forms an immediate link with the romantic. In the early thirties the perfect feminine room was described as having "low islands of light" that would give a feminine quality of charm. It was also considered important to design spaces for "personal becomingness" corresponding to women's hair colors, that is, blondes, brunettes, and "fading beauties" (women over forty). For example, noonday blondes were advised against having walls of robin-egg blue; the moon blonde was told that she would be best suited to delicate French-style rooms and should surround herself with pale blues, greens, or mauves. The red-haired blonde was warned against, red, violet, and bluish crimson. The drab blonde, on the other hand, was described as essentially the best type because she would fit well into a sort of house that a man liked.

(Right) Emerald green satin covers the entry walls of this apartment designed by Dennis Abbé. (Opposite page) A hand-painted flamingo screen dominates one end of the glowing apricot-colored living room. (Photos: Ambrose Cucinotta)

Setting for a raven-haired beauty

This New York apartment is contemporary, although it appears to have been designed in the late twenties or early thirties. The single woman for whom this space was designed wanted her interest in art deco reflected in her environment. Designer Dennis Abbé, also an avid collector of art deco (see pages 40–41), accepted the challenge of creating a seductive feminine space.

If some parts of this apartment seem reminiscent of a luxury liner built during the thirties, it could be because many elements were found aboard an old liner and incorporated into the decor. For example, the rug in the entry of the apartment and the solid brass columns in the four corners of the living room were salvaged from the old ship.

Emerald green satin wrapped around hundreds of packing tubes and attached to the foyer walls duplicated the wall treatments found in many hotels in the thirties. The apricot-colored living room glows in the late afternoon and is accented by a large flamingo screen.

Entering the bedroom of this femme fatale is like walking into a garnet. The smoldering red ambience is reflected from every surface and is perfectly suited to the thirties' theory that a space should compliment its occupant. A chaise lounge glistens seductively against satin-covered walls. The ceiling is covered in quilted satin matching the bed and its half-tester. Garnet mirrors at the head of the bed reflect gazelles and mysterious tropical forms etched on the dressing table. The nostalgic thirties echo in every part of this very feminine room.

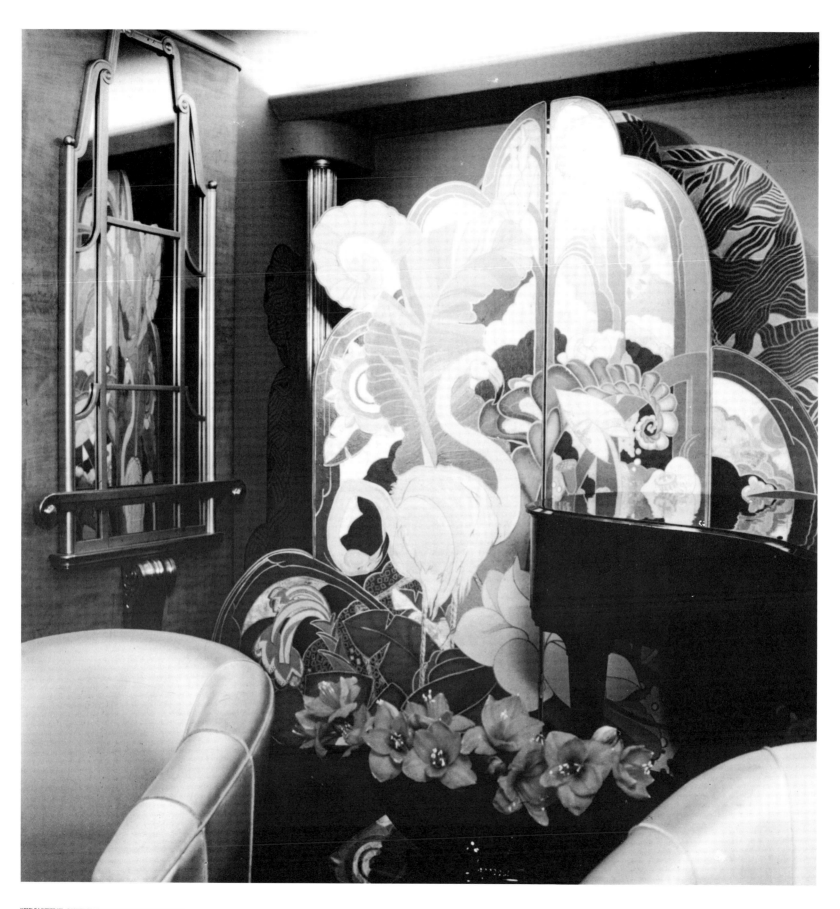

Art deco pieces
are set off
against green satin
wall treatment.
(Photo: Ambrose
Cucinotta)

Cozy seduction

The shimmer of crystal and silver against a sophisticated dark background betrays the complexity of the woman who resides here. Her carriage and movement reveal that she is a retired model, who had become subdued while nurturing a large family. Suddenly, at midlife she found herself facing a single lifestyle. Seeking to regain some of her former identity, she enlisted the services of professional designer Doris Bruno to change her living environment to reflect her altered lifestyle.

This home has the quality of very skillfully blended perfume. The varied fabric textures are like the fresh top notes and the cozy feeling is like that of deep woody base notes. The spaces are held together by the whimsical contrast of very simple fabrics used with such very opulent textures as furs. It is simultaneously innocent and sophisticated—and therefore seductive. Note how the library only increases the desire to know more about the owner of the books.

This home also has several afterglow spaces (see Chapter 10). The breakfast area with its cozy country atmosphere and the sitting room on the second floor are such spots. Wondering about the bedroom? Sorry, discretion dictates that it be left to your imagination.

The dramatic entry foyer forecasts the unusual spaces within designed by Doris Bruno. (Photo: Richard Milgate)

(Opposite page) Soft inviting seating areas with multiple small patterns make cozy seductive spaces. (Above) This breakfast room is a perfect afterglow space for lovers. (Left) Amidst fur throws, opulent fabrics, and soft lighting, this second floor sitting room is a perfect spot to cuddle on cold evenings. (Photos: Richard Milgate)

Seductive sensuality

High-intensity seduction is difficult to maintain. Overdone it can become boring and cease to seduce, but combined with a touch of the romantic and a hint of the sensuous, it can indeed be provocative.

This desert home designed by James Callahan combines the best of all three types of spatial eroticism. Large black sensuous vases and seductive lighting create a sense of mystery that lures you into the space. The hypnotic whirlpool of light on the ceiling is cast by large crystal globes placed on low tables. The dark carpeting and two tortoise finish walls of the living room are reflected in two mirrored walls. Tropical banana leaves set against a large circular acrylic arc and the statue of an ancient fertility goddess add exotic romantic elements to the space. Decanters on a shelf behind the bar highlight the sensuous quality of the liquor and add to the sparkling glamor.

(Above) The custom-designed bar area is made highly seductive with glittering lights and well-placed mirrors by designer James Callahan. (Right) Entry into this seductive home is enhanced by the subtle combination of soft fabrics, a huge plant, and controlled lighting.

(Left) The desert valley is viewed through erotic tusks arched over a sculptured female bust. (Below) Though this living room appears low keyed, its ceiling of swirling light, primitive sculpture, and erotic black vases are clues to its seductive intent. (Photos: Sheldon Lettich)

Who said a kitchen cannot match the sensuousness of other areas in your environment? Because a dining table was placed at the far end of this area and it also opened to other spaces, it was designed to conceal most of the ordinary kitchen appliances. The refrigerator and a sink are the only elements that betray the identity of this space, and the angle of the custom-designed burl counter also serves to break the stereotyped kitchen look. Silver and china are stored in floor-to-ceiling cabinets on the rear wall. A butler's kitchen concealed behind closed doors adjoins this area and is used for serious cooking.

The juxtaposition of glittering seductive lights with romantic overtones is confined to the public areas of this home. A subtle shift in mood occurs as one enters the private romantic sanctuary. The sophisticated custom-designed bed has mirrors subtly placed at the head of the bed. An afterglow space on one side of the bedroom overlooks the pool and is ideal for quiet meals for two. The bedroom atmosphere is further enhanced by a view of the city lights framed by two huge tusks and a sensuous bust.

This home illustrates how the romantic, seductive, and sensuous can be blended into a very effective environment that remains exciting.

(Above) This sensuous area with its pale-cream-colored burl counters and mirrored base cabinets breaks all rules about how a kitchen is supposed to look. (Left) Callahan shifts to a more subtle use of mirrors and intensifies the textural content in this romanticly sensuous bedroom. (Opposite page) A private bedroom sitting area overlooks the pool and provides a place for sharing special moments. (Photos: Sheldon Lettich)

Romantic seduction

Your first view of the living room provides only small clues to the complexity of the space created by designer William Gaylord. Rather than being arranged in a stereotyped manner, the seating and tables are purposely placed to seductively lure a visitor to explore more of the space. The mirrored fireplace and the stainless steel alcove stacked high with rustic logs is typical of the textural contrast found throughout this home. Styles and periods also range from ultra-contemporary to ancient; note the Egyptian bust reflected in the mirror. It is the kind of space that can comfortably accommodate the removal or addition of any objects without it becoming less romantic or less seductive.

The bedroom duplicates this balance of seduction and romance. Another mirrored fireplace reflects the regal bed canopied in suede and covered in lynx fur. The glamorous bath through the doorway is completely finished in richly grained marble reflected into infinity by mirrors placed on two walls.

Below the townhouse a lush, private garden with a floating desk is reserved for secluded dining.

(Above) Designer William Gaylord set a secluded dining place in a lush garden. (Top) Dark brown suede covers the walls of this romantic bedroom. (Right) Mirrors reflect the brown marbled walls and floors of the master bath. (Opposite page) The furniture is seductively placed to lure one deeper into the space. (Photos: Jaime Ardiles-Arce)

Aphrodisiac Environments: Facts and Fetishes

In a never-ending search for methods of attracting the opposite sex we have devised many ways to make ourselves more exciting and enticing. This pursuit of ideal aphrodisiacs extends to the places we visit and the spaces we live in. When bachelors thought their pads would be able to replace foreplay, spaces had indeed been elevated to aphrodisiac status. In fact everything from traditionally romantic places like the seaside to singles bars and discos have become aphrodisiac spaces. Different seasons, such as springtime, have also been considered more conducive to arousing sexual interest. The bewitching hours of the night were also counted on to assist in erotic endeavors. Anything that we are able to touch, feel, smell, or eat has become a part of the frantic search.

Water: the immortal aphrodisiac

Water is one of the most powerful natural aphrodisiacs. Because our lives begin in the water of the womb, it seems appropriate for legend to have made Aphrodite, the Greek goddess of love, emerge from the sea at birth. Water, long associated with immortality, be-

Nero's wife firmly believed bathing in asses' milk produced soft skin. (Photo: Paramount Pictures, Claudette Colbert; Museum of Modern Art)

came incorporated in universal religious beliefs and has been used for centuries to cleanse away sins.

The Fountain of Youth has been sought as an answer to our eternal quest for health and beauty. When special minerals were found in natural hot springs, soaking in the water to improve the health became a wide-spread socially acceptable custom. Milk and other concoctions were used for beauty and the pure sensuality of the experience.

A scene from a 1941 film starring Claudette Colbert depicts the legendary bathing habits of Nero's wife. Every springtime she would bathe with fresh strawberries floating about the water. When the berries were out of season she bathed in the milk of asses, which, according to Roman custom, promoted sexual vigor. Its obvious success is evidenced by her refusal to travel without taking along fifty asses to provide the precious milk. For those who wish to concoct a milk bath a recipe is in Chapter 9.

After the fall of the Roman Empire public and private bathing ceased and everyone apparently accepted filth and personal body odor as a natural way of life. It was not until the Crusaders returned to Europe with tales of strange foreign customs from the Middle East that water was again appreciated for its sensuous use. The communal Turkish bath became the rage of twelfth-century Europe. In some regions these bath houses were called "stews," and in Italy they were known as "bordellos." Everyone, including monks and

nuns, flocked to bath houses. At first cleanliness appeared to be the motive, but it soon became evident that the patrons were simply enjoying the sensuous quality of "stewing" in the hot steam. It was only a matter of time, however, before someone realized that all this sensual enjoyment could be combined with sexual delights. Thereafter bath houses became very profitable for the ladies who ran them.

As the stews changed, spatial layouts were expanded to include ramps above the bathing areas where a gallery of observers could watch the fun. Beds were conveniently placed in the far corners of the large room, and the tubs were equipped with long boards that served as refreshment tables for the soaking patrons. It might indeed be a blow to realize that those princes and princesses of childhood fairy tales did not spend all their time in the castle. They may well have been part of the medieval cocktail hour shown on top of page 124. A hot tub with a floating table introduced in 1982 by the Kohler Company underscores the fact that design solutions are based on meeting basic human needs.

Eventually all the bath houses were closed, and for hundreds of years any form of tub bathing was considered a very suspicious and outrageous act of immorality. The taboo against bathing was reinforced by the myth that too much cleanliness was dangerous to one's health. A wash stand containing a basin and pitcher of water was placed in each bedroom for spot bathing and was considered

more than adequate for personal hygiene. Most people, including royalty, may have been totally submerged in water only once or twice in their entire lives—usually at birth and again on their wedding day.

Beliefs about the evils of bathing and its tendency to promote promiscuity accompanied the early American settlers. Colonial states such as Virginia and Ohio passed laws about the number of baths (usually not more than one) an individual would be allowed each month. A hundred years later some small private tubs began to appear, but only the wealthy could afford the price of the tub and the official permit required for ownership. One popular English model called a "slipper tub" would seem more aptly named a "straitjacket" because it was purposely designed for only one person.

In the midnineteenth century hundreds of tubs began to appear in homes all over America. By the Sexual Revolution hot tub stewing and group bathing similar to those medieval swinging parties had been revived. Because Americans enjoy the status of owning their own homes and their own cars, it was natural for them to want their personal hot tubs, as opposed to communal bath houses. Americans placed tubs above or below ground and in bedrooms, living rooms, small patios, roof-top penthouses, and even decks overlooking the ocean.

(Opposite page left) Medieval hot-tub cocktail hour patrons (top) seem remarkably similar to this contemporary group of party-goers (bottom). (Photos: Bettmann Archives: Kohler Company) (Opposite page right) Slipper tubs were designed to make group bathing impossible. (Drawing: Bettman Archives) (Above left) A glowing red outdoor jacuzzi was designed by Olivia Neece. (Photo: Sheldon Lettich) (Left) Seductive glittering reflections were designed by Jerry Ohrbach and Lynn Jacobson. (Photo: Mark Ross) (Above) Bathing in the luxury of a marble tub is an ancient custom. (Design: ASET for Marble Technics; photo: Bo Parker)

In the late seventies Kohler introduced its "Total Environment." This concept in sensory engineering offered a secluded retreat where cares, tensions, and fatigue would melt away in response to the invigorating elements of nature. The environment permitted the individual to be surrounded by warm sun, refreshing rain, cleansing steam, or soothing winds. Enjoyment was enhanced by the addition of wall paintings, or an aquarium could be installed in the wall. A complete audio system could provide music or the sound of waves, wind, or sea gulls. While no legal action has been taken to date against this sensuous environment, it would surely have been condemned as witchcraft by the medieval world.

(Left) Bubble baths are a timeless bit of seduction. (Source: Kohler Company) (Below left and right) The "Total Environment" developed in the late seventies by the Kohler Company made it possible to surround yourself with sun, wind, steam, and music.

Aphrodisiacs for seductive dining

If seduction is the goal of your dining experience, then you should consider the appropriate symbolism of the foods upon which you dine, as well as the place and time of your feast. If "we are what we eat," then we should put special emphasis on foods that are well-known aphrodisiacs. It has been thought that certain types of shell fish could lure "young virgins from their path," while other shell fish are known for their ability to increase male potency. Some men, for example, have been known to consume dozens of raw oysters to assure the success of their sexual conquests. It would also be appropriate to finish the feast with such fruit as figs or pomegranates—both thought to be the food of the gods and therefore capable of producing exciting results. Wine, of course, is a necessity at your seductive luncheon, and advice on selecting wines can be found in any good bookstore.

The site for eating such foods can be a picnic, a campfire, the seaside, a mountain top, or your own private hideaway. Time should stand still in the place you select for this special event. Day should move into evening without either of you being aware of its passing. The two dining areas shown on pages 127–128 illustrate how lighting and glittering surfaces can accomplish this effect. The seductive setting can also project a playful quality like the one on the right of page 129.

The traditional seductive luncheon that continued into late afternoon was made popular by those living in Mediterranean countries where it was customary to take a long afternoon siesta. A four-hour disappearance can become a bit difficult to explain in countries without this convenient timeout. But in any major city or small town there is usually a place where lovers can disappear. Perhaps a small hotel with a restaurant will offer the seclusion needed for those long luncheons. They should not be confused with three-martini (tax-deductible) luncheons or popular brown-bag openings.

Enjoy elegant dining amidst glittering crystal and mirrors. (Designer: Robin Roberts; photo: Tom Yee)

(Opposite page) Paul Rudolph designed a seductive circular dining area with mirrors, curved seating, and strips of lights in the floor. (Photo: Tom Yee)

(Left) The Touch Restaurant designed by Stanley Felderman features seductive art deco murals painted by Dennis Abbé. (Photo: David Glomb)

(Above) A playful seduction could take place on this "lips" couch. (Designers: Richard Ohrbach and Lynn Jacobson; photo: Mark Ross)

The bedroom as aphrodisiac

The bedroom has served as a cultural and political barometer that has registered the smallest shifts in custom and belief. For example, French royalty often held court in the fifteenth century while reclining in huge ("king-sized") beds. As the bed became symbolically associated with royal power its size increased until it reached gigantic proportions in the sixteenth century. The underside of canopies became highly eroticized. Many were decorated with explicit pictures painted or embroidered on expensive fabrics to increase sensual delights. King Louis XIV gave a detailed description of how a mirrored canopy that collapsed during a love session discouraged their use for a brief period.

When the French Revolution marked the demise of royal power the bed also declined in size and remained small until the Sexual Revolution. An American film made in the early nineteen-forties, appropriately entitled "Twin Beds," illustrates the state to which the bed had shrunk. Movie censors, charged with upholding the American image of the bedroom as a space designed exclusively for sleeping, would not allow a man and a woman to be filmed together in bed. To a great extent, this film was responsible for the popularity of the twin bed in American homes during the forties. This trend lasted well into the late 1950s and may have inadvertently prompted the start of the Sexual Revolution. By the midfifties a Rita Hayworth film entitled "Pal Joey" openly proclaimed the return to the aphrodisiac bedroom. Platforms, canopies, and entire ceilings with mirrors began to reappear. Almost 200 years after the French Revolution king- and queen-size beds regained status as the erotic altars of the Sexual Revolution.

(Above) The bed chamber of Empress Eugenie at Fontainebleau shows why we associate "king-sized" beds with royal power. (Drawing: Bettman Archives) (Right) The American 1941 movie "Twin Beds" shows how small they had become as moralists tried to disassociate the bed from anything erotic. (Photo: United Artist; Museum of Modern Art)

In the nineteen-eighties some major fears have surfaced about the future of the bedroom. Social scientists and psychologists became concerned about the "disappearing" bedroom. As the cost of housing and interest rates have risen, many people have been unable to afford large spaces, resulting in the trend toward smaller homes, one-room studios, and lofts. Very clever solutions have been designed to conceal beds in wall cabinets, under tables, and recessed into the floors of big city lofts, but the sense of security, sanctuary, and refuge of the bedroom has been lost.

(Left) A 1957 American film with Rita Hayworth predicted the return to large opulent beds. (Photo: Museum of Modern Art) (Above) New devices developed in the eighties allow a full-size mattress to be concealed in a very small space. (Source: Selig Inc.)

Newspaper headlines of the eighties reflected the rapid invasion of the bedroom by electronic devices. When television was introduced in the fifties there was serious concern about its effect on the American family, although many family members have been conceived by the flickering blue-white light of the eroticized television screen. Today there is an increasing trend to move the computerized work environment into the bedroom. Again researchers fear a decrease in intimate activities, which may cause mental health problems. Though there may be some cause for alarm, researchers have overlooked the fact that clothing, furs, jewelry, books, and televisions have been properly eroticized before being admitted into the sanctity of the bedroom. When the personal computer was declared "Man of the Year" by *Time* magazine in 1982, its eroticizing process was virtually completed.

Extremists tend to fear the prophetic forecasts made by popular science fiction movies like "The Alien." We may find beds transformed into individual electronically controlled cocoons where human larvalike occupants will be kept warm, receive sustenance, and perhaps even sexual stimulation from a computer "mother." Perhaps hotels of the future will provide similar sleeping arrangements.

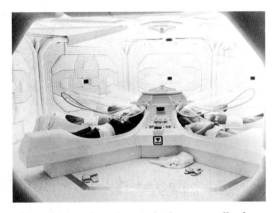

(Above) Some fear that as beds are totally de-eroticized they may become mere electronically controlled sleeping cocoons. (Photo: 20th Century-Fox "The Alien"; Museum of Modern Art) (Above and right) The bedroom is disappearing in American homes. (Designer: Don Chappel; photo: Tom Yee) (Opposite page) During the sixties and seventies beds were frequently recessed into the floor, thus making them a part of the open space design approach. (Designer: William Conti; photo: Tom Yee)

The bed as aphrodisiac

It is natural for the bed to have become a symbol of our longings for health, youth, and love. The shape, size, and placement of the bed have frequently been manipulated in the belief that different aphrodisiac effects would result. For instance, a belief in the healing and youth-giving quality of the damp foggy night air that rolls in from the Pacific created a West Coast craze in the thirties. Many film stars slept on the roofs of their homes. The picture on the right shows how beds—designed to operate like dresser drawers that could be rolled in and out—were incorporated into the roof of film star Ann Harting's Hollywood home.

The round bed was obviously considered an aphrodisiac by thousands of bachelors who made it standard equipment in their apartments during the sixties. It was replaced during the seventies by the water bed that had medically proven health benefits, as well as many exciting sensual and sexual delights.

Perhaps the least known, but most spectacular, aphrodisiac bed was developed by a Dr. James Graham in 1778. Like many other Englishmen of that period, he was deeply concerned with "magnetic vapours" and their possible therapeutic effects on treating certain physical and mental problems. Dr. Graham rented the bed out by the hour or longer if need be to those "happy persons who have the honour and the paradisical blessedness of reposing on it." This "celestial, medico, magnetico, musico, electrical bed whose seemingly MAGICAL influences were celebrated from pole to pole, and from the rising to the setting sun" guaranteed users "the removal of barrenness" and would "likewise improve, exalt and invigorate the bodily and mental faculties of the human species."[1]

Although no drawings or plans remain of his "Grand Celestial State Bed," Graham did offer detailed descriptions in many public lectures. They are reprinted here[1] for those who may wish to duplicate this marvelous bed.

[1]John Davenport, *Aphrodisiacs and Anti-Aphrodisiacs*, London, Luxor Press Ltd., 1869.

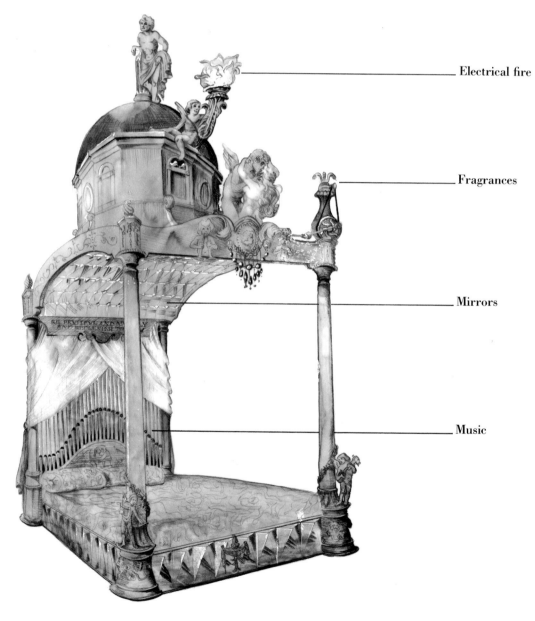

Electrical fire

Fragrances

Mirrors

Music

Grand celestial state bed

Size:

The "Grand Celestial State Bed! then, gentlemen, which is twelve feet by nine wide, is supported by forty pillars of brilliant glass, of great strength and of the most exquisite workmanship, in regard to shape, cutting and engravings; sweetly delicate and richly variegated colours, and the most brilliant polish!

Dome:

"The sublime, the magnificent, and I may say, the super-celestial dome of the bed, which contains the odoriferous, balmy and ethereal spices, odors and essences which is the grand magazine or reservoir of those vivifying and invigorating influences which are exhaled and dispersed by the breathing of the music, and by the attenuating, repelling and accelerating force of the *ELECTRICAL FIRE* is very curiously inlaid or wholly covered on the underside with brilliant looking-glass, so disposed as to reflect the various attractive charms of the happy couple, in the most flattering, most agreeable and most enchanting style. On the top or summit of the dome, are placed, in the most loving attitudes, two exquisite figures, representing the marriage of Cupid and Psyche, with a fine figure of Hymann behind and over them, with his torch flaming with *ELECTRICAL FIRE* in one hand and with the other, supporting a celestial crown, sparkling, likewise, with the effulgent fire over a pair of real living turtle doves, who, on a little bed of roses, coo and bill under the superanimating impulses of the genial fire! The other elegant groups of figures which sport on top of the dome—Cupids, the Loves and the Graces! Besides festoons of the freshest and most beautiful flowers, the figures have each of them musical instruments in their hands, which are made to breathe forth sounds corresponding with the appearance of the several instruments—flutes, guitars, violins, clarionets, trumpets, horns, oboes, and kettledrums.

Post:

"On the posts or pillars too which support the grand dome are groups of figures, musical instruments which in sweet concert with the other instruments, at the commencement of the tender dalliance of the happy pair, breath forth celestial sounds! Lulling them in visions of elysian joys! opening new sources of pleasure and 'untwisting all the chains which tie the hidden soul of harmony!'

Head:

"At the head of the bed, in the center front, appears sparkling with *ELECTRICAL FIRE*, through a glory of burnished and effulgent gold, the great, first ever operating commandment, BE FRUITFUL AND MULTIPLY AND REPLENISH THE EARTH! Under this is a most elegant and sweet toned organ, in the front of which is a fine landscape of animals and a wedding scene.

Mattress:

"In the celestial bed no feathers are employed; but sometime mattresses filled with sweet new wheat or cut straw, with the grain in the ears and mingled with balm, rose leaves, lavender flowers and oriental spices and at other times springy hair mattresses are used.

Sheets:

"Neither will you find upon the celestial bed linen sheets; our sheets are of the richest and softest silk or satin; of various colours suited to the complexion of the lady who is to repose on them. Pale green, for example, rose colour, sky blue, black, white, purple, azure and blue. They are sweetly perfumed in the oriental manner, with otto and odour of roses, jessamine, tuberose, rich gums, fragrant balsams and oriental spices. In short, everything is done to assist the ethereal, magnetic, musical, and electrical influences, and to make the lady look as lovely as possible in the eyes of her husband and he, in hers.

Magnets:

"But the chief elastic principle of my celestial bed is produced by artificial loadstones. About fifteen hundred pounds weight of artificial and compound magnets are so disposed and arranged as to be continually pouring forth in an ever-flowing circle inconceivable and irresistibly powerful tides of the magnet effluxion, which is well known to have a very strong affinity with the *ELECTRIC FIRE*.

"Such is a slight and inadequate sketch of the Grand Celestial bed, which being thus completely insulated and highly saturated with the most genial floods or *ELECTRICAL FIRE!* Fully impregnated moreover, with the balmy vivifying effluvia of restorative balsams and medicines and of soft fragrant oriental gums and pervaded at the same time with full springing tides of the invigorating influences of music and magnets gives each elastic vigor to the nerves, on the one hand, of the male, and on the other, such retentive firmness to the female; and moreover, all the faculties of the soul being so fully expanded, and so highly illuminated, that it is impossible but that strong, beautiful, brilliant, nay DOUBLE DISTILLED children, if I may use the expression, must infallibly be begotten."

(Opposite page top) In an effort to reap the benefits of the moist night air, Ann Harding, like many Hollywood stars of the thirties, built beds on her roof. (Photo: Bison Archives)

(Opposite page bottom) Dr. Graham's "Grand Celestial State Bed" of 1778 guaranteed delights to all who rented it by the hour. (Drawing by Ben Kann based on a Chippendale bed of the period)

9

Engineering Seductive Spaces

In the other sensory engineering chapters the physical aspects that distinguish the particular types of erotic spaces are discussed. Evaluating not only these physical elements, but our emotional responses to seductive settings will help us anticipate and eliminate problems associated with their design. The high failure rate of many bachelor apartments designed to seduce women proves that seductive spaces should be evaluated by those for whom the space was designed.

Seductive space evaluator

At one time or another we have either designed our own seductive interior or been lured into a space designed by someone else. Most people harbor distinct memories of their responses to those spaces. Although photographs cannot provide adequate information about all the sensory engineering elements in a space, such as fragrances and sounds, carefully chosen questions about the spaces can increase your awareness of particular cues that evoke positive or negative responses. Select a space from Chapter 7 that you found visually seductive and a second space that provoked a negative response, and answer the following questions about the

A beautiful life-sized version of the erotic Botticelli painting of Venus is reproduced on a screen. Any art of your choice can be reproduced by the La Verne Gallery.

spaces. If you are sharing living accommodations compare your answers with those of your partner.

1. Does the purpose of the space appear obvious?

2. Do you find the use of sparkling lights and glittering surfaces exciting?

3. Were romantic cues added to relieve the intensity of the seductive glitter?

4. Would you describe the space as mildly provocative rather than highly seductive?

5. Do you find the mirrors in the space intimidating?

6. Do the textures add to the seductive quality of the space?

7. Are you uncomfortable in a space that is obviously designed for one particular sex?

8. Is the art subtly suggestive or obvious?

9. Is a sense of playfulness created by spaces half hidden from view?

10. Would the space transform you into a femme fatale or a Don Juan?

SCORING: Give yourself ten points for every yes answer. If you score *10 to 20 points:* This space is not going to seduce you. In fact, you may feel trapped and start searching for the nearest exit. For a score of *20 to 40 points:* The interiors communicate seductive cues, but you feel ill at ease because the

seductive messages are too obvious. Scoring between *50 to 100 points:* You have found a space that will allow you to relax and become a full participant in the seduction scenario. You may even be tempted to act out your favorite seduction fantasy because the space has cues that make it romantically seductive. Since the spaces vary from room to room, the grand seduction can progress in any part of the space.

Universal seductive cues

Because seductive interiors serve as transition spaces between the romantic and sensuous phases, they frequently reflect cues of the other phases. This is clearly illustrated in the comparative table and the bar diagram shown on pages 138–139. Although this often makes seductive spaces seem elusive and difficult to analyze, their universal cues nevertheless are crucial to their function. Some of these cues are shown on the seductive tree diagram shown on page 140.

The apparent differences in male and female approaches to seduction further illustrate that the creation of seductive spaces is largely a matter of understanding what is considered seductive by those who are to be seduced. Some of the more obvious seductive cues include:

1. Abundant use of mirrors and other glittering surfaces.

2. Many sources of direct light, with the source of light (bulb) exposed.

3. Bright intense colors. The pink that was frequently used in romantic settings now become an intense red.

4. Numerous settings, such as seductive bathing and dining areas, for sharing the enjoyment of aphrodisiacs.

5. Circular shapes and forms, for example, round beds, tubs, chairs, and conversation pits.

6. Seductive fragrances, ranging from floral blends to spices, mosses, and sandlewoods.

(Right) This table lists the romantic, seductive, and sensuous cues used to create the seductive settings shown in Chapters 6 and 7. (Opposite page) The bar chart shows the range of cues that are listed in the table on the opposite page.

SEDUCTIVE SETTINGS* Chapters 6 and 7	ROMANTIC ELEMENTS	SEDUCTIVE ELEMENTS	SENSUOUS ELEMENTS
1. Disco		Colors: bright, intense Sparkling light sources	
2. A Romantic Disco Fantasy	Views of city Nature: trees, plants, rocks Fantasy: animals Rustic furniture	Intense light sources Sparkling mirrors	
3. Some Things Speak for Themselves	Plants: banana leaves Fireplace	Glittering mirrors Bar: glittering glasses	Satin bed Lines of sofa Satin pillows
4. Dazzling Seduction	View of city	Colors: bright, intense Sparkling light sources Mirrors	Black backgrounds Darkness
5. Mood-Altering Space	View of city View of water: sunset Location: height Piano	Colors: intense Sparkling lights Pillows on floor	Spiral stairs Vase texture/shape
6. Provocative Seduction		Symbols: phallic Sparkling light sources Pillows on floor	Voluptuous pillows
7. Setting for a Raven-Haired Beauty	Nostalgia: art deco	Colors: bright, intense (bedroom)	Satin fabrics
8. Cozy Seduction	Nostalgia: time, place Furniture forms Fabrics: floral prints	Animal fur on floor, furniture	Black background
9. Seductive Sensuality	View of city Ancient symbols: tusks, animals Plants Water fountain	Sparking light sources (public areas, bar) Mirrors Animal fur	Lines in furniture Textures
10. Romantic Seduction	View of city Nostalgia: furniture Art objects Plants Fireplace	Mirrors Animal fur Large mirrored bath/ whirlpool	Smooth leathers Smooth chrome/marble

Note: This evaluation is based on the visual elements in the photographs. It does not include factors such as music, fragrance, changes in lighting that could intensify the seductive atmosphere or make the space more exciting and enticing.

SEDUCTIVE SPACES*	ROMANTIC	SEDUCTIVE	SENSUOUS
Space 1		▆	
Space 2	▆	▆	
Space 3	▆	▆	▆
Space 4	▆	▆	▆
Space 5	▆	▆	▆
Space 6	▆	▆	▆
Space 7		▆	▆
Space 8	▆	▆	▆
Space 9	▆	▆	▆
Space 10	▆	▆	▆

*Note: Spaces that span one or more categories of erotic spaces will be the most successful in meeting your changing moods. Readers may identify additional elements based on personal preferences.

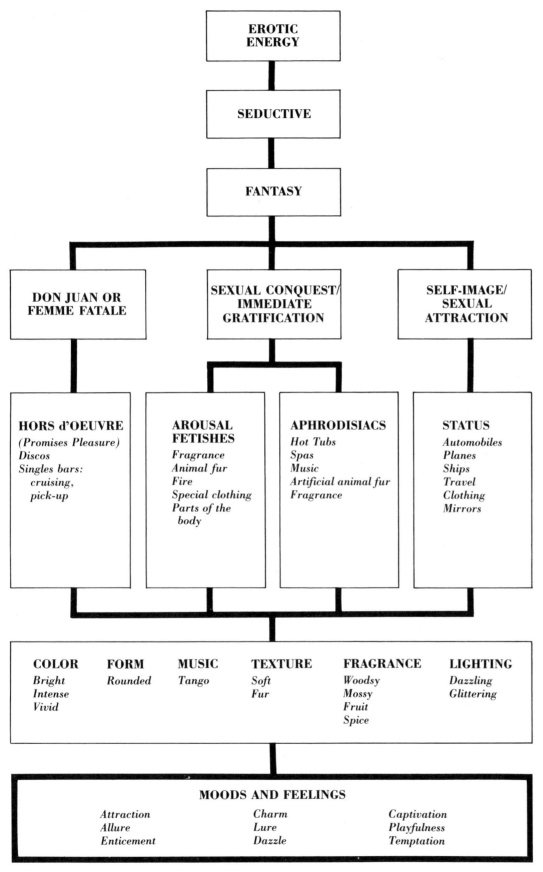

Furnishings, accessories, and textures

Because seductive spaces represent a transition phase between the romantic and sensuous, furnishings and accessories shown in any other phase can be used. For example, romantic four-poster beds draped with opulent fabrics can be transformed into beds unmistakably designed for no-nonsense sex. Many are equipped with ceiling mirrors and numerous electronic controls that regulate everything from the bedside. Beds used in seductive spaces may be king-sized, round, and occasionally filled with water. The Italian custom-designed bed shown on the left of page 141 can be hand-carved in your own image or the image of your beloved.

If your space is too small for a large round or canopied bed the Mombasa mosquito net could provide the necessary combination of mystery and seduction that you are seeking. The manufacturer of this seductive aphrodisiac describes hundreds of letters received from women who attribute their successful seductions to this netting. One woman in England requested an additional black net to use on special occasions. Three months later she ordered a smaller version in a natural color for a baby crib.

The seductive tree diagram (read from top to bottom) gives the many components needed to create a seductive environment. Note its relationship with the erotic wheel on page 16.

(Left) Want a bed that is uniquely yours? Have Italian artisans hand-carve your profile into the headboard. (Source: La Verne Gallery) (Above) A Mombasa net could be fitted over a bed or couch for the ultimate seductive effect. (Source: Youngjohann Hillman, Inc.)

There are some pieces of furniture that are considered standard equipment in seductive settings. The history of the chaise longue is intertwined with many seductions. Until recent times, every woman's boudoir contained a chaise longue for resting in the afternoon.

A screen, whether large or small, is another seductive piece of furniture. In the Victorian era ladies slipped behind a shoulder height screen to change into something more comfortable while continuing a seductive dialog. The large screen shown on page 136 that features Botticelli's famous painting of Venus would be too tall for seductive flirting, but would be an ideal bedroom background.

Seductive symbols are evident in the collection of round objects shown on page 144. The round glass table top is set on a round glass base sandblasted with Egyptian lotus flowers that signify fertility and immortality. The glass fish sculpture behind the table and the large circular feather wall hanging are also fertility symbols. An animal tusk (real or artificial) is the strongest male power symbol. The erect tusk looming over the reclining female is high-voltage seduction. Other tusk forms have been curved in varying degrees to form supports for tables, desks, and mirrors on page 145.

Seductive atmospheres. Backgrounds, lighting, music, and art are some of the most important elements to consider in engineering the seductive environment. For those who prefer the scenic route, entire walls and ceilings can be covered in mirrors. The paradise mirror rimmed in an electric turquoise recaptures the ancient symbolism of the circle. The male/female symbols of the Bird of Paradise flowers sandblasted on the surface create seductive tensions. The mountains in the background of the mirror intensify the message. For those who desire more overt seductive backgrounds, the erotic wall coverings shown on the facing page depict lovemaking in cultures from opposite parts of the globe. Sculpture by artist Arnold Goldstein also shown on the facing page captures pent-up passions in the highly charged seductive "Embrace."

(Opposite page top and bottom) Play out your favorite seduction fantasy on a chaise lounge. (Top: designer: Peter Rocchia; source: Wicker Works. Bottom: source: Roland Kentfield, Ltd.) (Left) Tantalizing subtlety best describes this foil-coated wallcovering. The movements of the Oriental lovers create intriguing patterns. An occasional glimpse of a human limb combined with flowing robes produces a delicious sense of mystery. For the agile, trim, and physically fit who like a challenge, this wallcovering will offer endless delights. The Roman scenes should also prove interesting to historic furniture devotees. (Below) The seductive "Embrace" is captured by artist Arnold Goldstein.

(Opposite page) The contrasts among smooth shiny glass, feathers, and animal fur produce all the seduction a single room could handle. (Source: Versailles Collection) (Left) This collection of tusks commands seductive attention. (Source: Versailles Collection) (Above) The paradise mirror reflects romantically seductive scenes. (Source: Farallon)

Aphrodisiacs. Wine is known as a delicate substance whose quality depends on loving care every step of the way from the vine to the moment of uncorking. Although you may not have a dusty wine cellar, there are portable wine storage units available to store your wine collection at the ideal temperature and humidity needed for proper aging.

No seductive setting would be complete without the aphrodisiac qualitites of water. The nostalgic brass-bottomed tub and the two whirlpool baths shown on pages 147–148 each make excellent settings for long hours of seductive lounging.

If you wish to duplicate some decadent ancient Roman bathing customs described in Chapter 8 here are some recipes:

For a *love bath* mix honeysuckle, jasmine, fuchsia, and carnation flowers. Allow to blend a few hours before dropping them into your bath together with a hot mixture of red clover, deer tongue, and orange peel. This is recommended for extended soaking with a friend.

For a special celebration try a *strawberries and champagne bath*. Mix one-half cup of freshly mashed strawberries into one-half cup of powdered oatmeal, one teaspoon Borax, and ten drops of strawberry oil. Place these ingredients in a tea bag and immerse in the bath water. Pour one cup of champagne in the bath, and save the remainder of the champagne for you and your partner.

For a light, playful *chocolate milk shake bath* combine two cups of fresh milk with two tablespoons of sesame oil and ten drops of chocolate oil. Shake well and pour under full force of running water. Jump in while the bubbles are still abundant.

For a *summer wine bath*, combine one cup of white wine, one tablespoon rosemary, one teaspoon of ground ginger, and ten drops of jasmine oil. Cover the container and store in the refrigerator for twenty-four hours. Strain and add to the bath water. In the winter port can be substituted for white wine.

For the final touch of elegant bathing seduction, have your towels warmed on the gold-plated towel warmer shown on the top of the facing page.

(Opposite page top) A sleek cabinet conceals a television set. (Source: Devin, Inc.) (Opposite page bottom) An electronically controlled wine cellar should be a part of every romantic setting. (Source: Cellar Masters.) (Left) Warm towels add that necessary touch of luxury. (Source: Myson, Inc.) (Below) Whirlpool bath by Jacuzzi creates relaxed moods.

Summary

Engineering for seductive settings requires you to develop insights about your emotional and physical needs and those of your partner. Seductive spaces should be transitional and therefore should exhibit romantic and sensuous cues as well as those that are seductive. Allow the space to evolve without following rigid rules to encourage maximum participation.

(Left) A very nostalgic brass bottom tub. (Source: Brass Bottoms, Inc.) (Below) Whirlpool bath by Jacuzzi enhances seductive moods.

PART FOUR

SENSUOUS INTERIORS

10

From High-Voltage to Afterglow Spaces

High-voltage sensuality cannot be attained without a smoldering period. Romantic and seductive phases are necessary preludes that prepare us to yield freely to the pleasures of sight, sound, smell, and taste. Once our sensory awareness level reaches this peak, we are able to enjoy the sensual world around us.

Sensuous spaces are designed to enhance our indulgence in and gratification of the erotic. They are touching spaces that offer physical comfort, opulence, and luxury.

How sensuous spaces differ from other erotic spaces

Dress designers have always provided women with excellent visual means of expressing eroticism. It is therefore easy to draw parallels between erotic spaces and women's evening gowns. A typical romantic gown, reminiscent of times past, would be made of a white organdy trimmed with lace and ruffles. A gown designed of glittering sequins with a thigh-revealing slit would be seductive. The sensuous gown could be made of satin that would cling to the body without exposing flesh.

If that sensuous gown were made of white

This organic cave environment designed by Barbara D'Arcy was equipped with the sounds of sea gulls and is an example of romantic sensuality. (Source: Bloomingdale's)

satin it would provoke *romantic sensuality*. If the gown were made of heavy natural linen that hung straight from the shoulders to the floor leaving us to guess at the form beneath, it would provoke *intellectual sensuality*. If, however, it were made of black satin, it would provoke *passionate sensuality*.

Romantic sensuality. The spaces most frequently termed "sensuous" are those having curved and undulating forms. These forms personify what is universally acknowledged as sensuality. The term "romantic sensuality" is used here to show its links to idealized forms found primarily in nature. The sensuous stair built of Kasota stone on the right of page 152 illustrates both undulating curves and a columnar curve beautifully combined in a Manhattan penthouse.

Romantic sensualists also desire a wide range of textures in their surroundings. The satin-covered bed shown on page 102 is another example of a romantic sensuous form. The bed's bulbous forms, constrained by tight-fitting white satin, begs to be caressed. An emotionally yielding environment is a sensual delight to the self-indulgent.

Intellectual sensuality. There are a large number of people who associate sensuality with bourgeois taste. Opulent luxurious spaces are considered decadent and lacking in spirituality. Yielding to sensual indulgence without intellectual control is considered destructive to moral and intellectual pursuits.

Therefore intellectual sensualists surround themselves with space that is sparce, angular, restrained, and austere. Less tactilely oriented than the romantic sensualist, the intellectual sensualist finds visual pleasure in structural purity that epitomizes the form follows function theory. Remaining aloof from mundane objects, the intellectual sensualist spends a lifetime of emotional restraint.

Passionate sensuality. The passionate sensualist uses space as a means to an end. If you have ever closed your eyes to block out distractions when trying to savor a beautiful memory, you will understand this type of space. All extraneous distractions must be removed if a space is to provide a setting for achieving sensual gratification. This is often accomplished by creating an almost totally black environment. Known to silence the most boisterous, this noncolor provides a spell-binding background for humans and their possessions. While the sparks created by passionate sensualists are set off in this setting, a black space is not for the security-loving romantic sensualist or the intellectual who would not be able to logically determine the distance from the door to the corner of the room. Black creates endless space that frightens those searching for a visual answer to a tactile question. But passionate sensualists love worldly pleasures, have a huge sexual appetite, and enjoy touching.

The following projects show examples of the three types of sensual spaces.

(Above) Intellectual sensuality places an emphasis on sparse angular space. (Designer: Adam Tihany; photo: Mark Ross) (Right) Romantic sensuality is embodied in this undulating curved stair designed by Bray-Schaible. (Photo: Jaime Ardiles-Arce)

I love it, but I wouldn't want to live there

Black is exciting, but the thought of living in a black space is incomprehensible to many. Perhaps black spaces elicit fear because we remember the fear of the dark as a child. We may also associate black with the void created when we are suddenly thrust into darkness by a power failure. On the other hand, there are brave people who welcome the qualities of black. Designer Phyllis Morris recalls how the novelist Harold Robbins requested a totally black study for his Beverly Hills mansion. He explained that the black space would remove distractions and help him concentrate on the paper in his typewriter.

It is this type of visual deprivation that New York designer Eric Bernard occasionally uses to encourage his clients to get in touch with their fantasies. By removing all extraneous distractions, he is often successful in helping his clients forget their preconceived ideas about space. Instead of conforming to the latest "fashionable look" they are convinced will impress their friends, Bernard attempts to expand their visual experiences.

Not only is black valued for its ability to remove distractions and create an unusual setting for people and their possessions, black is also treasured for its ability to allow changes in mood. Using his own apartment, Bernard demonstrated how a black space can change moods and feelings as often as you may desire. In fact, any environment designed with a noncolor background such as white, gray, and black may be totally changed. Black, however, is the noncolor that tends to erase all spatial imperfections and can provide an excellent background for your most sensual fantasies.

Passionate sensuality removes visual distractions to allow total concentration on one or two sensual elements. These black rooms by designer Eric Bernard explain the concept. (Top) The black room becomes decked out for spring with a huge bouquet of pastel flowers. (Right) The same black room changes character when the intense red of Christmas poinsettias is added. (Photos: Billy Cunningham)

Public sensuality

Most high-voltage passionately sensuous environments designed as touching spaces are usually found in intimate private spaces. Although movie theaters rely on black or darkness to provide primarily audiovisual stimulation, these spaces do encourage an abundance of public touching. In settings where we tend to dine, however, touching is usually confined to the food upon the palate.

F. Scotts', a restaurant in Palm Springs, California, designed by James Callahan, is quite the opposite. This restaurant is deeply erotic. The glamor of the main dining areas is enhanced by the use of mirrors, deep rich colors, and sleek sensuous forms that make touching everything in sight imperative. It is high-voltage, no-nonsense sensuality that would be too intense for a budding romantic relationship. The popularity of this restaurant must be attributed to the erotic needs of many mature relationships.

(Top) Large black erotic vases dominate this Palm Springs restaurant. (Right) James Callahan sets highly erotic forms and textures against a black background. (Photos: Charles S. White)

Shifting sensuality

Sensory engineers such as Eric Bernard have an incredible ability to control responses to an interior space. The qualities about black that tend to frighten are the same qualities that attract and excite us. One does not expect to find an indoor-outdoor fusion of space in a penthouse apartment. But the living room of this New York apartment unexpectedly forces our vision out to the city beyond. At night when the space is used for frequent parties, it seductively hangs suspended above the glittering city. During the daylight hours attention can be directed inward and all emphasis placed on a particular art object or a special floral arrangement. Most sensuous spaces cautiously filter nostalgia that might clutter our emotions. The only hints of nostalgia allowed are those linked to other eras such as art deco, which also produced sensuous objects. Although the textures vary from smooth leather on the seating to a rough ceiling, no individual texture commands complete attention in this room.

A comparison of the city landscapes shown on this page illustrates how skyscrapers, not unlike mountains, are transformed by the first rays of the morning light and continue to change throughout the day. In the bedroom the use of black is reversed from the background to a high-contrast accent against the buff-colored walls and floor. The designer has skillfully shifted the visual emphasis from exterior to interior by using the colors of the buildings as they look in the morning sun.

(Left) In early evening the buildings shift from buff to gray black. Designer Eric Bernard skillfully reversed the bedroom background colors to contrast with the skyline. (Above) The buff-colored city skyline seen during the morning offers a contrast with the black interior. (Overleaf) The living room of this New York penthouse is designed to shift your vision from the interior to the exterior. (Photos: Jaime Ardiles-Arce)

Subtle sensuality

Another penthouse high above Manhattan has many qualities that make it appeal to a large number of people—it is romantic, seductive, and sensuous all at the same time. The living room is angled and all midtown Manhattan becomes the focal point of the space. The interior space, pared down to offer little distraction from the vast city below, relies on sensuality to create a romantic setting.

The bedroom is mirrored on one wall to reflect the night scene and the ceiling represents a compromise between husband and wife. The husband wanted mirrors over the bed for the enjoyment of love-making. His wife felt intimidated at the prospect. The designers, Kenneth Brian Walker and Rick Manchen, suggested a louvered aluminum ceiling that not only reflected but also distorted. The couple found that the broken images were actually more erotic and stimulating than those provided by a conventional mirror.

(Bottom) A view of Manhattan at dusk serves as a subtle background for the romantic sensuous space designed by Rick Manchen and Kenneth Brian Walker.

(Below) The ceiling treatment successfully solved a difference of opinion between the husband and wife regarding a mirrored ceiling. (Photos: Jaime Ardiles-Arce)

Passionate sensuality

The concepts of passionate sensuality are evident in these spaces designed by Clive Wilson. As one dines in this elegant setting, the entire world can be blocked out. Complete concentration on the tastes, aromas, colors, and textures can be experienced in true epicurean tradition.

In another area of this home the bedroom offers a quiet retreat designed for savoring sensual delights. The light brown suede walls combined with the soft glow of brass and the warm luster of old wood provide a variety of textures.

The bath clearly illustrates another example of how black can be used to unify a very small space and force the contents to receive special attention. The designer understood Rembrandt's technique of placing people and objects against a dark background. Seen in this contrast all colors become glow like precious jewels and humans seem to radiate a special quality.

(Above right) Designer Clive Wilson created a bedroom with rich sensuous textures and carefully selected accents. (Right) All objects become jewel-like when set against a black background. (Opposite page) Dining in the manner of a passionate sensualist. (Photos: David Glomb)

Royal sensuality

What does a member of the Saudi royal family require in a sensuous bedroom? In this home, one of four scattered about the world, the owner required storage space for 300 pairs of shoes and seventy suits, a complete bar, and a compact kitchen. The tactile quality of the materials and surfaces was very important to the owner. Because the owner requested that only silks were to be used throughout, raw silks were used for the upholstery and refined silk satins were used for the bedding. All colors and forms were to reflect the sea.

Starting with the concept of "A Thousand and One Nights," designer Charles Burke planned a room that would simulate a starry night—like sleeping under the desert sky. The lights in the ceiling twinkle, glow brighter or dim, and also undulate to music. It is difficult to tell where the lights of the valley below end and the interior stars begin. The same undulating quality of the sea was carried out in the furniture shapes. The sofas snake across the space while the curving fireplace and the circular dais with its round bed carry the movement throughout.

Behind the sofa on the left a circular glass wall encloses a shower. This is strategically located to heighten sensual pleasures from all parts of the suite. The adjoining tub is rimmed in a black granite splash with padded walls above. This provides acoustic privacy and a good background for the music piped into the space. The sinks are made of concave granite with silver and stainless steel hardware.

As in other homes designed by Burke, the bedroom chamber is well hidden. It is located somewhere along a 40-foot hall concealed behind sculpture and black mirrors. Entry can be gained only by submitting the correctly coded computer numbers. Other automated elements include the fireplace that can be ignited and the desired flame height controlled electronically. The bath can also be drawn at any predetermined time. In addition the drapery, audiovisual elements, security equipment, and the twinkling stars above are controlled from the bedside. The blue neon sculpture is located behind the headboard and is reflected in the curving walls above the sculpture by a large beveled mirror 12 feet long that opens electronically to reveal a beautiful hidden garden with a fountain and ferns that can be enjoyed while lying in bed. This bedroom has become such a sensual delight that the owner has been known to linger for three or four days.

(Below) The round bed on the circular dais combined with the round fireplace and thousands of tiny lights twinkling above produces romantic sensuality. (Opposite page) Designer Charles Burke filled this entire room with undulating curves, sensuous surfaces, and many universal romantic cues. (Photos: Toshi Yoshimi)

Cool sensuality

Eric Bernard designed this cool gray apartment for a single woman. The penthouse exudes romantic sensuality. The public spaces of the home are designed in a series of radiating circles. Regardless of where one stands in this series, some architectural or decorative detail leads the eye back to the center living room area. For instance, the patterns of the antique art deco floor tiles used in the dining area serve this purpose.

The center living room, recessed below the surrounding areas, has custom-made circular seating upholstered in velvet. The silver leaf installed on the ceiling and some of the walls provides a soft hand-rubbed luster that casts a subtle contrast on the other textures in the room. This entire area produces a sensuous background for the enjoyment of art, music, and people.

The sensuous elegance of the public areas continues into the bedroom. A painting above the bed is aglow with the warmth of sunlight and blazing flowers. Partly reflected in the silver leaf inset above the bed, the room is clearly dominated by the painting and the bed. Everything that could possibly distract from the total sensuality of the space is electronically controlled from the bed. For example, the television can be raised and lowered into a storage area under the window.

(Above right and right) Eric Bernard designed a special mechanical device that electronically controls the television from the bed.

(Opposite page) The living room, circular in shape, has custom-designed seating and the soft shimmer of a silver foil ceiling. (Photos: Peter Vitale)

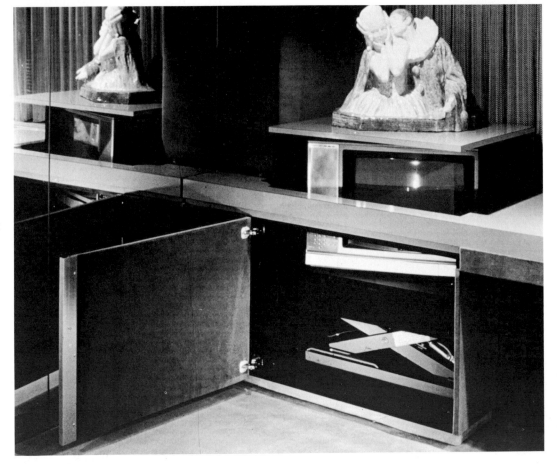

(Right) The radiating circles seen through the open areas of this penthouse are repeated in the dining area, which is slightly elevated above the living room. (Below) A painting with warm red-orange hues focuses attention on the bed area. (Photos: Peter Vitale)

Restrained elegance

At the beginning of this chapter the elegant undulating stair located to the right of the entry of this penthouse was used as an example of romantic sensuality. Turning away from the overwhelming opulence of this pink stone stairway, one is confronted by partial-pyramidal forms that are diametrically opposed to the shape of the stairway. Although the angular stone formations do not reach to the ceiling, the direction of their slant and their invasion of the space with pointed corners cause the forms to retreat and advance upon us simultaneously. Were it not for their pale pastel color they would indeed become ominous fortresses. These intellectually sensuous forms literally defy human touch, but once on the other side of the geometric forms we are rewarded with cozy seductive seating areas.

The bed in the master bedroom is positioned to take advantage of two magnificent views of the city. The decor is kept simple to allow the enjoyment of erotic sculpture and paintings strategically placed about the room.

Designers Robert Bray and Michael Schaible succeeded in creating an unusual juxtaposition of romantic and intellectual sensuality, combined with occasional seductive cues.

(Above) Visual privacy in the living areas is secured by partial pyramidal forms made of pink stone. (Below) Bray and Schaible designed semisecluded seating areas on the other side of the pyramidal forms. (Photos: Jaime Ardiles-Arce)

Crisp space

This space designed by architect Adam Tihany proves that less is more. With intellectual restraint, the environment is pared down to the bare essentials for living, while still providing the luxury and opulence found in sensuous spaces. This is accomplished, to a large extent, by visually removing the ceiling. Painting the ceiling black throughout the apartment visually changed the walls from support elements to screens between spaces. This illusion is amplified by the shoji screen-like door that separates the open living area from the bedroom area and the addition of an actual screen behind the couch. Another shoji screen used to divide the bedroom from a small study again increases the feeling of a ceilingless space.

In the living room all textures are kept relatively smooth and the furniture sparse but adequate. The audiovisual equipment is built into the wall without any attempt to hide its function, thereby making the knobs, levers, and glass of the television screen a part of the total space concept. The entire apartment is designed in noncolors black and white. Even the art is kept colorless. Therefore, the addition of any color into the space instantly arouses a sensuous level of awareness.

Adam Tihany believes that his responsibility as a designer does not extend beyond providing architectural elements and a few basic pieces of furnishings. He further believes that the neutral backgrounds he creates will allow the client freedom to expand on the idea by adding his or her own artifacts. Note that this concept has been expressed by most of the other designers of sensuous spaces in this chapter.

(Above right) Architect Adam Tihany painted the ceilings of this apartment black, thus making the walls seem to terminate visually in midspace. (Right) In this restrained elegant space the use of such noncolors as white, black, and beige makes the addition of any single color, whether of a flower or a pillow, immediately appreciated. (Photo: Mark Ross)

Romantic sensuality

Owning great art places a responsibility on its owners. Like exquisite jewels, these artworks demand an appropriate setting. In this home the owners, as well as the art, seem perfectly matched to this romantic setting.

When the owners purchased this home, built sometime in the late twenties, it was still in its original form. It lacked adequate lighting and had a closed-in feeling. The entry had openings to the dining room on the left and the living room on the right. At the far end, French doors opened to a portico that overlooked the city. This portico was supported by soaring Corinthian columns.

To open the space and provide a sensuous sweeping vista, designer Leza Lidow removed the French doors and extended the interior to include the portico. The original exterior Corinthian columns can be seen at the end of the new foyer. To find a sense of height that was needed for the art, a portion of the foyer ceiling and a room above were removed to provide the setting for the rare Indian art housed in that area. In the foyer near the entry the original ceiling was retained but mirrored to continue the same sense of height gained in the portico area.

Secure in their own personal identities, the owners selected art for their foyer that most people would only dare display in their most intimate surroundings. Below the erotic work of Italian painter Tomaso Ferroni a Lidow postage-stamped nude mannequin reclines on an Oriental table. A Gandhara Buddha surveys the grouping. The ease with which all this art is juxtaposed provides an irresistible sensuality.

To the right of the entry the stairway area was also transformed into a light and airy space for art. Below the new stairs is a three-piece wooden group sculpture by Melier. In the confessional a priest patiently listens to a woman knitting a garment as she performs her religious obligation. To the left is a tenth-century temple fragment from India. Two Jay Stussy paintings dominate the stair landing and a Saski painting is on the upper left wall.

In this romantic sensuous interior tensions are produced, not as the result of mechanically controlled lights or sounds, but by the powerful eroticism expressed in the art.

(Above) The entry foyer contains many pieces of rare erotic art reflected in the mirrored ceilings. (Right) This 1920s Bel Air, California, home was renovated by designer Leza Lidow. Inadequate lighting and a closed-in feeling were overcome by removing the French doors and enclosing a portion of the large portico. (Opposite page) The Corinthian columns that supported the portico became a part of the interior, which now houses a rare Chinese bronze collection. (Photos: Toshi Yoshimi)

*(Above) The original
stairway area was
dark and unused.
(Right) To the right of
the entry a sensuous
stair area was created
to house more of this
unusual art collection.
(Photo: Toshi Yoshimi)*

A way of life

A totally responsive environment that answers every mood, feeling, and physical need of the owners was created in an existing home by designer Charles Burke. Knocking out a large portion of the exterior wall allowed the spectacular, dome-covered circular bath to become an extension of the bedroom. Neon tubing installed in the dome of the bathing grotto is computer programmed to simulate the changing colors of the sunset. (Note the dome's different colors in the various photographs.) On either side of the bath entry are his and hers grooming alcoves that contain 14-karat gold-plated sinks and vanities.

Once the couple retreats to this luxurious sanctuary they are free to spend many uninterrupted hours. The amenities that make this possible are a bar, refrigerator, freezer, microwave oven, tape machine, audiovideo system, and a concealed 5-by-8-foot screen. The bed, located directly opposite the bath, serves as control center for the many operable elements in the room. The drapery, the bronze vertical blinds in the bath, as well as the sliding pocket doors at the bath entry may be opened and closed from controls at the bed. Dimming devices regulate lighting in the bath, as well as the outdoor lighting. Via telephone they can communicate with anyone at the outside entry doors and supervise the entire security system. Like concealed doors in Renaissance European palaces, the bedroom entry door is hidden. Only those who know the combination to the computerized wall panel located outside the bedroom can gain entry.

The unique bathing grotto deserves a closer look. The 2300-pound hand-sculptured seating area that surrounds the circular whirlpool tub is specifically designed for safety and ease of entry. Additional seating is provided along each side of the grotto. Controls to operate the blinds and lighting are also located near the tub. The design illustrates that all the personal requirements of clients may be met by skilled sensory engineers.

(Above) When this home was purchased by new owners, designer Charles Burke was hired to renovate it. The addition of a bath suite represented a major part of the work. (Left) Construction was required to create the bath suite.

(Top) A circular domed bath added to one side of the bedroom contains hand-carved circular seating. (Above) The rim of the star-filled dome contains additional lighting needed to wash the dome in colors matching the owners' moods. (Right) Concealed doors can totally close off the bath from the bedroom. (Photos: Toshi Yoshimi)

Afterglow spaces

In a world of hors d'oeuvre environments, aphrodisiac settings, and touching spaces that promise us excitement, glamor, and ⸻ afterglow spaces promise nothing ex⸻ ⸻disturbed stretches of time, ⸻eone else. They are ⸻ ⸻n in order

⸻s ⸻ull

⸻orld ⸻o de⸻ ⸻e dif⸻ ⸻y men ⸻that we ⸻sign two ⸻assics of

⸻e involved ⸻ntle down⸻ ⸻natural out⸻ door s⸻ ⸻ning stream. Water is continua⸻ ⸻rough aluminum pipes imbedded int⸻ ⸻earth-colored

(Top) Paul Rudolph, architect, designed this romantic sensuous bath for a woman. The sound of running water can be heard as it circulates through aluminum tubes on the surface of the floors. A skylight in the copper dome creates a soft golden light. (Right) The bath Rudolph designed for a man has many of the same features, such as a copper dome, but the addition of exercise bars and fewer organic design elements make this different from the female space. (Photos: Tom Yee)

carpet. The natural landscape concept is enhanced by the addition of smooth rocks and soft sponges strategically positioned to allow contact with bare feet. The low partition in the center of the room shields the bidet. A skylight centered within a copper dome allows a restful golden glow to wash the entire space. The large luxuriant tub and a screen for viewing films placed nearby produce an irresistible setting for relaxation. A contoured reclining lounge attached to the wall provides a place to read or enjoy the sunlamps installed above. Circular storage containers are placed along one wall and on another end a makeup counter was surrounded with small round mirrored disks that simulate a sparkling water surface.

Although the bath designed for the male was organic in form, it did not attempt to simulate the romantic natural setting provided for the female. The large skylight highlights the circular trapeze exercise bars placed directly under the dome. Copper sheeting is used both in the dome and throughout the space. A raised platform that runs along one wall contains the tub and also houses recessed storage.

Lights concealed in the bottom of a circular pit built into the center of the floor are reflected in the soft copper color of the walls and ceilings. Intended to simulate the warmth of glowing coals in an open campfire, it provides an inviting place to relax. When the pit was not in use it was covered with an exercise pad. A dressing area is to the rear.

In designing these two baths, the architect addressed what he considered to be feminine and masculine needs. That is, the more contemplative nature of the female and the more active interest in body building on the part of the male. Only a decade later it is interesting to note how many woman share an equal interest in body building.

(Above) Compare another view of Rudolph's sensuous bath for a woman with the more austere bath for a man (opposite page). (Right and below) Drawings by Brotman illustrate the location of the major fixtures in the woman's space (right) and the man's bath (below).

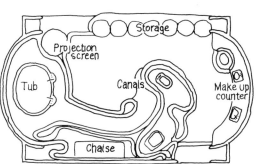

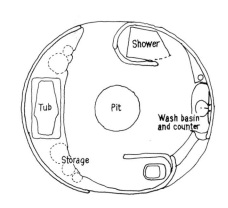

Not limited to this chapter, other afterglow spaces can be found in sitting or dining areas within the bedroom like the one shown in Chapter 7 on page 119. A cozy breakfast area seen on the top of page 115 also serves as an afterglow space. An afterglow space can also be a terrace overlooking the Golden Gate Bridge in San Francisco Bay. Wherever you choose to celebrate your afterglow, those spaces should provide a restful retreat needed to recharge your batteries.

(Opposite page) A Palm Springs patio was designed by Insights, Inc. to be shared by partners. (Photo: David Glomb) (Below) An ideal spot for afterglow dining, this patio setting designed by William Gaylord overlooks San Francisco Bay. (Photo: Jamie Ardiles-Arce)

11

Engineering Sensuous Settings

The types of sensuous spaces shown in Chapter 10 include those that display romantic undulating curves, spaces based on an intellectual approach to form and function, and passionate spaces that blackout spatial clutter. To determine your sensuous spatial needs make use of the sensory space evaluator below.

Sensuous space evaluator

Pick one space that you found appealing and apply the questions to that space. Answer the questions a second time in relation to a space you may have found disturbing. Comparing your responses to both spaces should help you pinpoint what attracted you to one and repelled you about the other.

1. Did the space make you want to reach out and touch someone or something?

2. Does the space provide a welcome relief from visual clutter?

3. Did you want to take off your shoes and feel the texture of the floor?

4. Did the space make you suddenly aware of any new shapes?

5. Would you feel out of place in the space?

A detail of the Donghia sofa shown on the top left of page 185 illustrates that each superb curve and fold is engineered for sensual enjoyment.

6. Would you have trouble keeping the space free of plants?

7. Would the sparseness of the space disturb you?

8. Did the curved forms make you feel sexy?

9. Did a lack of varied color disturb you?

10. Would the space hold your interest?

Scoring: For each yes answer give yourself 10 points. If you scored *10 to 40 points:* You enjoy having a clutter-free environment because your highly charged mind cannot categorize feelings and emotions when too many visual elements interfere. You must feel in control of your space at all times. No deceptions, mysterious shadows, or unknown surfaces should be allowed. You enjoy the background surfaces of your space without unnecessary textures or embellishments. You are proud of being able to control your environment through superior intellectual sensuality.

Scoring *50 to 70 points:* A space devoid of curves and rich textures would make you very uncomfortable. You are capable of enjoying a wad of paper on the floor or a desk stacked with papers. You would welcome a room filled with art and allow each piece to communicate in its own way. You welcome the unexpected joy of a changing environment regardless of how minute the change may be. You are a romantic sensualist.

If you got between *80 to 100 points:* You

enjoy creating high-contrast settings for the objects around you. Your spaces make people and things glow with richness. Even though you do have dramatic control over your space, you allow it to flow with your emotions. No detail of your environment goes unnoticed, even the parts that may be shrouded in darkness are frequently reflected in mirrors to double your enjoyment. You want to share your intense emotions because you are a passionate sensualist.

Universal sensual cues

When a selected number of sensuous spaces from the preceding chapter were evaluated for universal cues in the accompanying table, it was interesting to find that like romantic and seductive spaces, some sensuous spaces also contain universal cues typical of the other types of erotic spaces. For example, Royal Sensuality (pages 160–161) contains romantic and seductive cues. This illustrates that spaces having a broader spectrum of cues better serve those using the spaces because they allow for changing moods. The bar chart on page 181 corresponds to the spaces shown on the table and visually clarifies the comparisons among them.

As you review the visual cues table, many similarities of the sensuous should become evident. For example, most sensuous spaces are created with noncolor backgrounds that allow the sensualist to fill or not fill the spaces as desired. The general moods and feelings that are frequently associated with sensuous spaces are summarized in the tree diagram shown on page 182. (Read from top to bottom.) The tree diagram illustrates how individual sensuous elements relate to each other and contribute to the overall sensuous atmosphere. Although spontaneous and intuitive responses are essential to the enjoyment of sensuous spaces, these responses are not found in rigid intellectual sensuality. Are we then to conclude that intellectual sensuality is really a pseudo type of sensuality? Or does intellectual sensuality perhaps reveal fantasies about established wealth and cultural superiority?

Increasingly popular examples of intellectual sensuality are evident in bachelor apartments of the eighties, which, as the Sexual Revolution has waned, have gradually shifted to more subtle backgrounds in which to display male-oriented power symbols (see Chapter 7). These backgrounds are commonly based on an all-white decor or the gray-flannel-chrome-and-glass look that signals the desired cues of old wealth and cultural elitism.

The problem of a chrome-and-glass person finding happiness with a romantic (mentioned in Chapter 7) was poignantly brought out in a recent article about a couple's search for sleek, uncluttered happiness. Married to a man who insisted that she let go of personal attachments and resist the temptation to save sentimental objects, she was urged to be brave enough to live in sparse spaces. Feeling deprived of the objects that had always filled her life and given her environment a lived-in look, she struggled not to bring plants and other decorative items into the apartment.[1]

Paul Rudolph's design concept for a male and female bath over a decade ago reveals his intuitive understanding of the female's spontaneous response to organic romantic sensuality (pages 173–175). The bath designed for the male has curved forms, but it is more sparse and has fewer undulating cues found in nature.

When designing sensuous spaces remember that the goal is to provide a background against which the sensuality of two people can be fulfilled.

[1]Carol S. King, *Designers West*, February 1983.

SENSUOUS SETTINGS* Chapter 10	ROMANTIC ELEMENTS	SEDUCTIVE ELEMENTS	SENSUOUS ELEMENTS
1. Shifting Sensuality	View of city Art deco art	Mirrors	Black leather Emphasis on textures Sculpture
2. Subtle Sensuality	View of city	Mirrors	Emphasis on shapes Dark bedroom walls
3. Passionate Sensuality	View of city Color	Sparkling lights Mirrors	
4. Royal Sensuality	City lights Stars Fireplace	Sparkling lights Mirrors	Undulating sofa Circular bath/bed
5. Cool Sensuality	View of city	Silver leaf Glass surfaces	Touching surfaces: gray velvet Art
6. Restrained Elegance	Soft colors	Concealed seating Mirrors in ceiling	Degree of sparseness Angular mixed with romantic curved stair
7. Crisp Space			Simple backgrounds No distractions Intellectual sparseness
8. Romantic Sensuality	Columns	Mirrors	All distractions removed Intellectual
9. A Way of Life	Stars in dome	Sparkling lights Mirrors over bed	Round bath/other curved areas
10. Afterglow Space: A Woman's Bath	Nature: organic	Glittering surfaces Mirrors	Undulating curves Organic forms

*Note: This evaluation is based on the visual elements in the photographs. It does not include factors such as music, fragrance, changes in lighting that could intensify the sensuous atmosphere or make it more romantic or seductive.

SENSUOUS SPACES*	ROMANTIC	SEDUCTIVE	SENSUOUS
Space 1			
Space 2			
Space 3			
Space 4			
Space 5			
Space 6			
Space 7			
Space 8			
Space 9			
Space 10			

*Note: Spaces that span one or more categories of erotic spaces will be the most successful in meeting your changing moods. Readers may identify additional elements based on personal preferences.

(Opposite page) The romantic, seductive, and sensuous cues used to create sensuous settings shown in Chapter 10 are listed in this table. (Left) The bar chart illustrates the range of cues listed in the table on the opposite page.

The sensuous tree diagram (read from top to bottom) lists the many components needed to create a sensuous environment. Compare this with the erotic wheel on page 16.

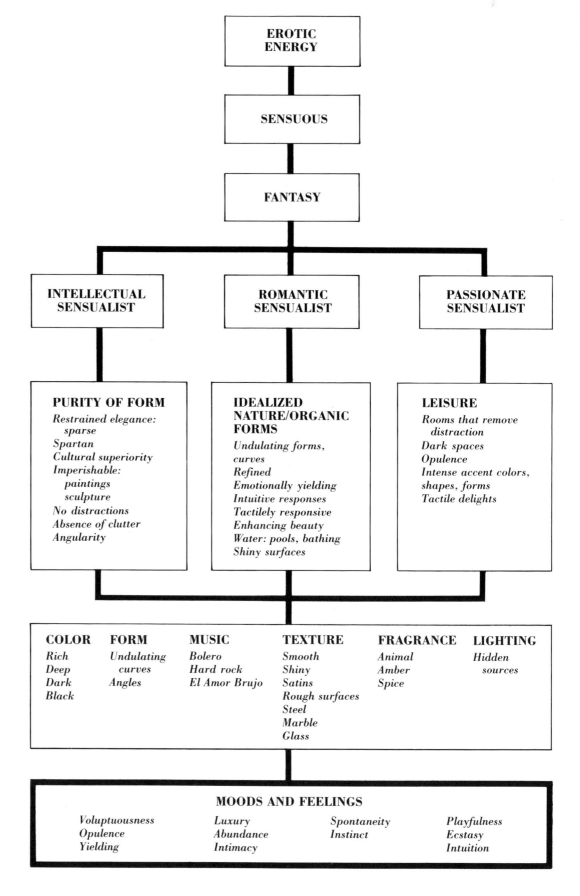

EROTIC ENERGY

SENSUOUS

FANTASY

INTELLECTUAL SENSUALIST	ROMANTIC SENSUALIST	PASSIONATE SENSUALIST

PURITY OF FORM
Restrained elegance: sparse
Spartan
Cultural superiority
Imperishable: paintings sculpture
No distractions
Absence of clutter
Angularity

IDEALIZED NATURE/ORGANIC FORMS
Undulating forms, curves
Refined
Emotionally yielding
Intuitive responses
Tactilely responsive
Enhancing beauty
Water: pools, bathing
Shiny surfaces

LEISURE
Rooms that remove distraction
Dark spaces
Opulence
Intense accent colors, shapes, forms
Tactile delights

COLOR	FORM	MUSIC	TEXTURE	FRAGRANCE	LIGHTING
Rich	*Undulating curves*	*Bolero*	*Smooth*	*Animal*	*Hidden sources*
Deep	*Angles*	*Hard rock*	*Shiny*	*Amber*	
Dark		*El Amor Brujo*	*Satins*	*Spice*	
Black			*Rough surfaces*		
			Steel		
			Marble		
			Glass		

MOODS AND FEELINGS

Voluptuousness	*Luxury*	*Spontaneity*	*Playfulness*
Opulence	*Abundance*	*Instinct*	*Ecstasy*
Yielding	*Intimacy*		*Intuition*

Furnishings, accessories, and textures

When reviewing the wealth of sensuous objects designed for the home, it becomes evident that emphasis is placed on the pure sensuous enjoyment of natural materials such as exotic woods, marble, crystals, silk, and semiprecious stones. Other hard-surfaced furnishings are made from smooth reflective materials such as chrome, glass, or acrylic.

Beds: Sensuous beds are sleek and have simple lines and forms that create an efficient use of space and assure the physical comfort of those using the bed. Many are designed as platforms while others, like the Italian bed shown on the right, have tilting headboards and bedside trays that swing around to make dining in bed more comfortable.

The one-of-a-kind solid brass bed shown below should answer the needs of the intellectual sensualist who craves luxurious materials and simplicity of form. Though extremely sophisticated in design, a hint of fantasy is evident in its altarlike appearance.

(Above right) Sleek Italian-designed bed with adjustable headboard comes with swiveling side tables. (Source: B & B America-Stendig) (Right) A one-of-a-kind solid brass futuristic platform was designed for a pure sensualist. (Artist: Ellen Finn)

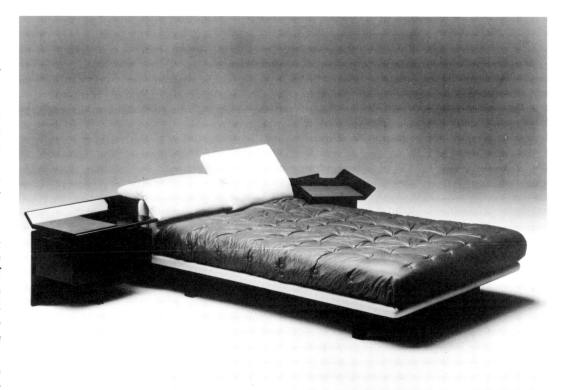

Seating: In sensuous settings seating usually follows bodily forms, creating gently undulating furnishings. Some seating like the "Aphrodite" rocker shown below is hand carved of beautiful wood. Other upholstered seating is most voluptuous and inviting, like the sofa in raw silk shown on the facing page. The bulbous curving forms of the silk sofa by Donghia are pure romantic sensuality (see facing page and page 178). Every detail of its construction invites visual enjoyment.

(Below) A rocking chair fit for an Aphrodite. (Source: Michael Coffey) (Opposite page top left) Donghia combines opulence of shape, form, and texture to produce a romanticly sensual sofa. (Opposite page top right) John Mascheroni designed this luxurious seating for sensuous spaces. (Source: Swaim Originals) (Opposite page bottom) Curving romantic sensuality is evident in this seating by Breuton.

Tables: Tables used in sensuous environments are frequently constructed of very elegant transparent materials that do not visually distract from other objects in the immediate area. Whether made of glass or acrylic, the tables shown on pages 187–188 project a special sensuous presence in the spaces they occupy. When marble and chrome are combined, the weight of the marble seems suspended in space on the reflective chrome base (see top page 188).

Other marble tables have gentle flowing forms like the console table shown on the right. The accompanying tusks are tactilely inviting accessories. The cabinet shown below is designed of rich oiled mahogany and stainless steel.

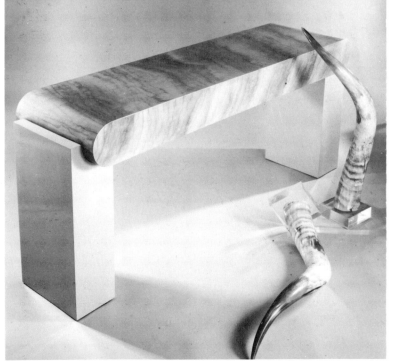

(Left) The unadorned natural beauty of marble is captured in this console table by James DiPersia for Avento. (Below) All sensualists can delight in the beauty of this mahogany and stainless steel buffet by Paul Evans Studio. (Opposite page) Romantic sensuality glows from within a sanded acrylic dining table designed by Nella Longari for Casa Nova.

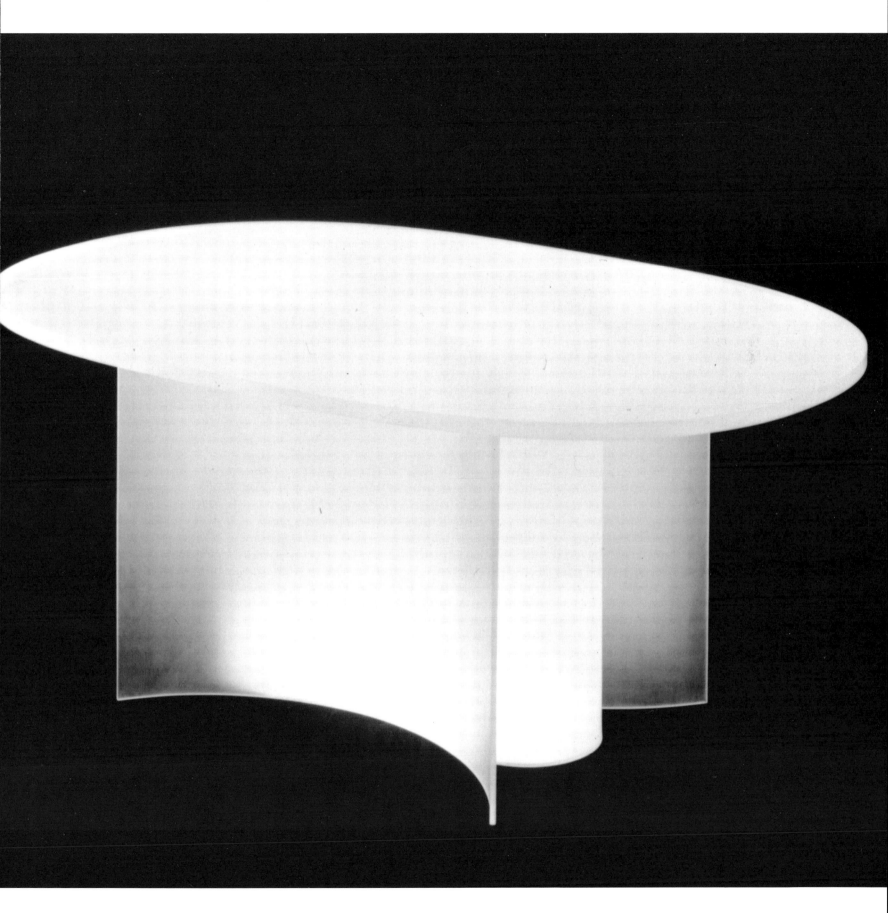

(Right) Polished marble sits atop a circular chrome base that includes storage space by Paul Evans Studio. *(Below)* Cool sleek acrylic "Mirage" card table was designed by Donghia for Paul Associates.

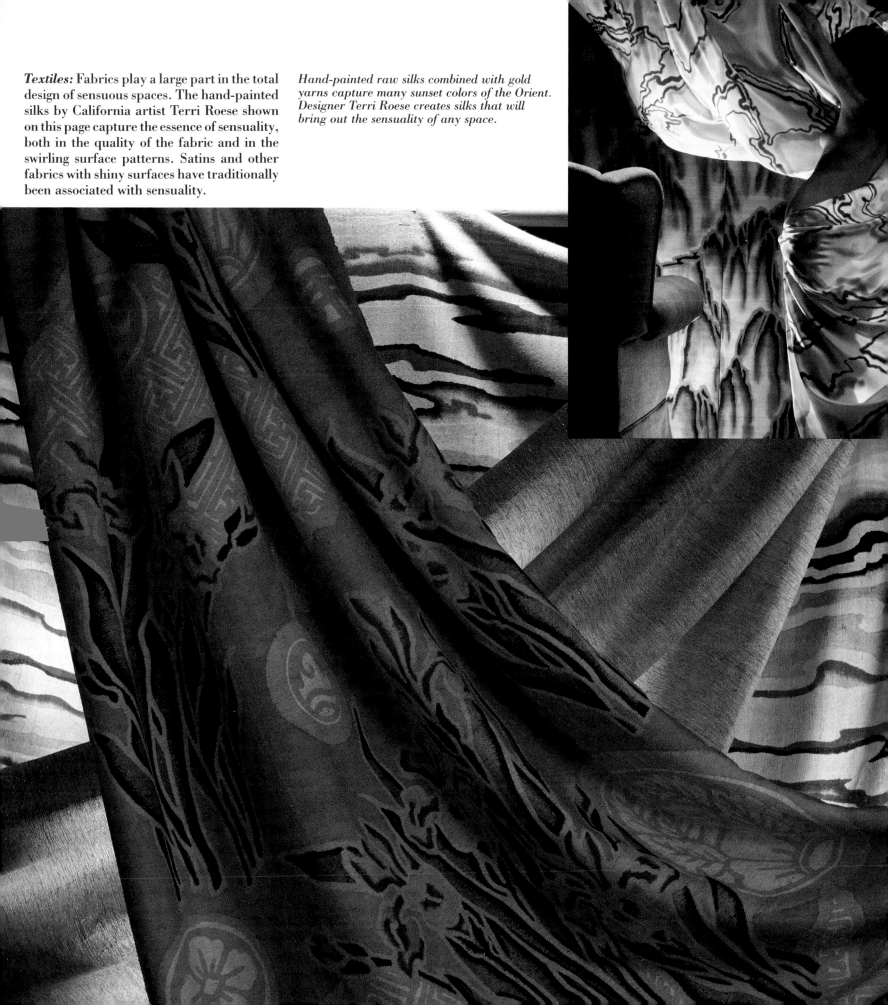

Textiles: Fabrics play a large part in the total design of sensuous spaces. The hand-painted silks by California artist Terri Roese shown on this page capture the essence of sensuality, both in the quality of the fabric and in the swirling surface patterns. Satins and other fabrics with shiny surfaces have traditionally been associated with sensuality.

Hand-painted raw silks combined with gold yarns capture many sunset colors of the Orient. Designer Terri Roese creates silks that will bring out the sensuality of any space.

Accessories: The translucent quality of glass is used not only on tables but in vases and beautifully hand-blown lamp shades. Organic in form, the containers magnify the beauty of dried or live flowers. A brass sculptured table lamp shown below is a perfectly balanced serpentine form.

(Below) This brass serpentine sculptured table lamp is designed in a limited edition by Casella Lighting. (Right above and below) Hand-blown saline etched Venetian glass creates soft sensuous lighting. (Designer: Alfred Barbini; source: Ogetti) (Opposite page) Sensuous glass containers designed by Italian designer Alfred Barbini extend visual enjoyment beyond the surface. (Source: Ogetti)

Bath fixtures: The major difference between a sensuous bath and those shown in the romantic and seductive sections is its utter simplicity and opulence of materials. Fixtures shown below are made from malachete, and real gold faucets are not uncommon. Other semiprecious stones, such as tigereyes and crystal, are incorporated into faucet handles. Chrome is also fashioned into sensuous faucets, and glass is used to make a gracefully curved spigot.

(Below) The beauty of the semiprecious malachete counter and gold-plated faucets and wash basin designed by Sherle Wagner would bring great joy to any sensualist. (Opposite page) If mirrors and marble add to your sensual enjoyment a bath designed by Richard Ohrbach and Lynn Jacobson should help you attain sensual highs. (Photo: Mark Ross)

(Top left) Based on three cubes, a chrome spout arches sensually in a high turn as it emerges from the center cube while the levers thrust from right and left cubes. (Source: Paul Associates) (Top right and below) The "Primo" and "Jetset" faucets designed by Stanley Paul achieve complete unity of form and function. Both the hand levers and spout are an integral part of the geometric concept. (Source: Paul Associates) (Opposite page top left and right) Faucet handles for sensuous baths can range from pure crystal balls to brass circles within circles designed by Artistic Brass. (Opposite page bottom left) For the intellectual sensualist who loves geometric shapes, Sherle Wagner uses semiprecious malachite and tigereye to create this 2000 series of bath accessories. (Opposite page bottom right) Raymond Jurado's design combines the sensuality of three materials: a stainless steel counter, a black marble counter top, and a pure silver basin. (Source: Paul Associates)

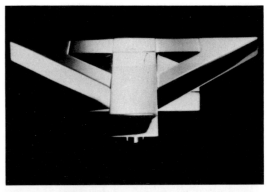

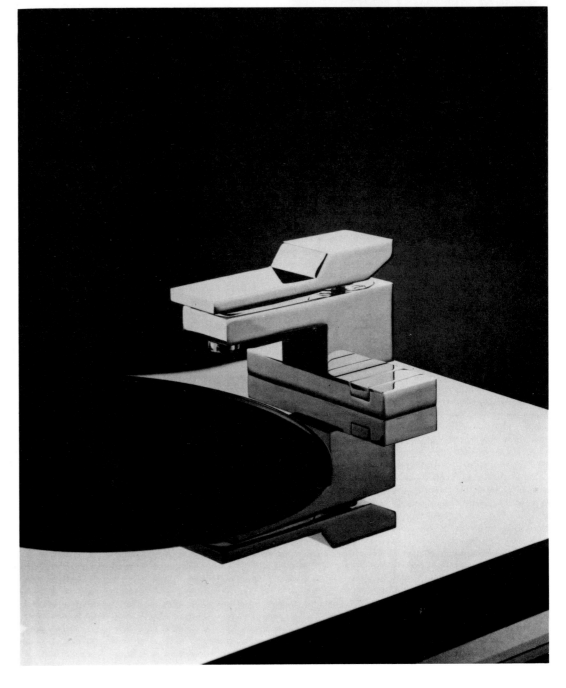

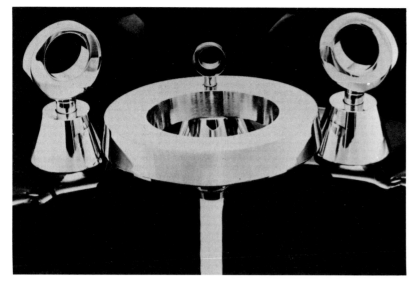

"La Vasca Tonda" is the ultimate bath and shower in the round. Surrounded by panels of Plexiglass one can enjoy the heated towel bars, hand-held sprays, a full-length mirror, and an eight-jet whirlpool system. (Source: Hastings Tile and Il Bagno)

Selected Bibliography

American Psychiatric Association. *A Psychiatric Glossary.* Washington, D.C., 1976.

Brusendorff, O., and P. Henningsen. *A History of Eroticism.* New York: Lyle Stuart, Inc., 1966.

Calas, Douglas and Elena. *Icons and Images of the Sixties.* New York: E.P. Dutton and Company, Inc., 1971.

Carlton, Michael. "How 'Suite' Life Can Be at Only $2,500 a Night," *Dallas Times Herald*, March 1982.

Cavendish, Richard, ed. *Man, Myth and Magic.* Vols. 1–24. New York: Marshall Cavendish Corporation, 1970.

Chesler, Phyllis, and E.J. Goodman. *Women, Money and Power.* New York: Morrow, 1976.

Cohen, Daniel. *Re-Thinking.* New York: M. Evans and Company, Inc., 1982.

Dullea, G. "Making Way for the Bedroom Invasion," *The New York Times*, 1982.

Dinnerstein, D. *The Mermaid and the Minotaur.* New York: Harper and Row, 1977.

Eddings, C. "Men's Fragrances Taking Lead in Order of Innovation," *Daily News Record*, December 1978.

"Fall Safe Toppling Redwoods Spur Cagey Solution" (Associated Press), *Arizona Republic*, February 1983.

Fitch, R.E. *The Decline and Fall of Sex with Some Curious Digressions on the Subject of True Love.* Westport, Conn.: Greenwood Press, 1957.

Frankfort, E. *Virginal Politics.* New York: Quadrangle Press, 1972.

Frazier, G. and B. *The Bath Book.* San Francisco: Troubador Press, 1973.

Freud, Sigmund. *Beyond the Pleasure Principle.* New York: Bantam Books, 1967.

Friedl, E. *Women and Men: An Anthropologist's View.* New York: Holt, Rinehart and Winston, 1975.

"From Bedroom to Boardroom, Romance Novels Court Changing Fancies and Adorable Profits," *Time*, Apr. 13, 1981.

Gilligan, Carol, "Why Should a Woman Be More Like a Man," *Psychology Today*, June 1982.

Giovannini, Joseph. "Sex Stereotypes in Design," *The New York Times*, December 1982.

Glasser, William, M.D. *The Identity Society.* New York: Harper and Row, 1972.

Goffman, Erving. *Relations in Public: Microstudies of the Public Order.* New York: Basic Books, Inc., 1971.

———. *Stigma, Notes on the Management of Spoiled Identity.* Englewood Cliffs, N.J.: Prentice-Hall, Inc., 1963.

Goldberg, Ellen. "Valentine, Let's Hear It for Pay-Attention-to-Love Day," *The Boston Globe*, 1983.

Goldberg, Herbert. *The New Male: From Self-Destruction to Self Care.* New York: Signet Books, 1979.

Goldberg, Robert M., Ph.D. *The Encyclopedia of Human Behavior: Psychology, Psychiatry and Mental Health.* Vols. 1–2. Garden City, N.Y.: Doubleday and Company, 1970.

Gorney, Roderic, M.D. *The Human Agenda.* New York: Simon and Schuster, 1973.

Greer, G. *The Female Eunuch.* New York: McGraw-Hill, 1971.

Groddeck, Georg. *The Book of the It.* New York: Vintage Books, 1949.

Gutman, Robert, ed. *People and Buildings.* New York: Basic Books, 1972.

"Here Comes Country Chic," *Newsweek*, Aug. 16, 1982.

Hill, Langdon. "Hard Times Keep Romance Alive," *Tempe Daily News*, Apr. 17, 1983.

Hille, Judy. "Romancing the Reader," *Arizona Republic*, January 1982.

Houck, Catherine. "All Those Lonely Men (in Bars)," *Cosmopolitan*, August 1971.

Hutton, Ginger. "What Does a Man Look for in a Woman?," *Arizona Republic*, June 1982.

Huxtable, Ada Louise. "The Troubled State of Modern Architecture," *Architectural Record*, January 1981.

Janeway, Elizabeth. "The Woman's Movement," in *Comprehensive Textbook of Psychiatry, Vols. 1–3.* Baltimore, Md.: Williams and Wilkins Company, 1980.

Johnson, E. "Bloom, Gloom or Doom," *Perfumer and Flavorist*, June–July 1977.

Jung, Carl G. *Man and His Symbols.* New York: Dell, 1964.

Kaplan, Freedman, and Sadock. *Comprehensive Textbook of Psychiatry.* Vols. 1–3. Baltimore, Md.: Williams and Wilkins Company, 1980.

Kazan, J. "What Smell Success?," *The Working Woman*, November 1982.

Key, W.B. *Subliminal Seduction: Ad Media's Manipulation of a Not So Innocent America.* Englewood Cliffs, N.J.: Prentice-Hall, Inc., 1973.

Knight, R.P. *Sexual Symbolism.* New York: The Julian Press, Inc., 1957.

Lambert, H.H. "Biology and Equality: A Perspective on Sex Differences," *Signs*, April 1978.

Lasch, Christopher. *The Culture of Narcissism.* New York: W.W. Norton and Company, 1978.

Lee, Susan. "Lonely? No Hope at Health Clubs," *The New York Times*, March 1982.

Lipton, Lawrence. *The Erotic Revolution*. Los Angeles, Ca.: Sherbourne Press, Inc., 1965.

Luce, Gay G. *Body Time*. New York: Pantheon Books, 1971.

Lynch, Kevin. *What Time Is This Place?* Cambridge, Mass.: MIT Press, 1972.

Maccoby, E.E., and C.N. Jacklin. *The Psychology of Sex Differences*. Palo Alto, Ca.: Stanford University Press, 1974.

Male, Emile. *The Gothic Image*. New York: Harper and Row Publishers, 1958.

Marcuse, Herbert. *Eros and Civilization*. New York: Vintage Books, 1955.

Mayer, Barbara. "A Man's Bedroom Is His Castle," *Arizona Republic*, July 1980.

Mehrabian, Albert. *Public Places and Private Spaces*. New York: Basic Books, Inc., 1976.

Miller, J.B. *Toward a New Psychology of Women*. Boston Beacon Press, 1976.

Montague, Ashley. *Touching*. New York: Columbia University Press, 1971.

Mooney, Elizabeth C. "Beginning Marriage with a Splash," *American Way Magazine*, September 1981.

Mumford, Lewis. *The Pentagon of Power: The Myth of the Machine*. New York: Harcourt Brace Jovanovich, Inc., 1964.

Naisbett, John. *MegaTrends*. New York: Warner Books, 1982.

Oldenberg, Ramon, and D. Brissett. "The Essential Hangout," *Psychology Today*, April 1980.

Ploss, Herman H. *Women in the Sexual Revolution*. New York: Medical Press, 1964.

Post, Emily. *The Personality of a House: The Blue Book of Home Charm*. New York: Funk and Wagnalls Company, 1930.

Proshansky, Harold, William Ittelson, and Leanne Rivlin, *Environmental Psychology: People and Their Physical Settings*. New York: Holt Rinehart and Winston, Inc., 1976.

Reik, Theodor. *Sex in Men and Women: Its Emotional Variations*. New York: Farrar, Straus and Cudahy, 1960.

————. *Of Love and Lust*. New York: Farrar, Straus and Cudahy, 1959.

Reuther, R., and E. McClaughlin. *Women of Spirit*. New York: Simon and Schuster, 1979.

Robin, Caytie. "A Computer Era, Lost Love in the Machine," *Arizona Republic*, February 1982.

Rosaldo, M.Z., and L. Lanphere. *Women, Culture and Society*. Palo Alto, Ca.: Stanford University Press, 1974.

Rvitenbkeek, Dr. Hendrik M. *The New Sexuality: New View Points*. New York: Franklin Watts, Inc., 1974.

Schilder, Paul. *The Image and Appearance of the Human Body*. New York: John Wiley and Sons, Inc., 1950.

"Sexual Revolution Losing Out to Boredom, Expert Says," *Arizona Republic*, October 1980.

Sherfey, M.J. *The Nature and Evolution of Female Sexuality*. New York: Vintage Press, 1973.

Simson, Otti Von. *The Gothic Cathedral*. New York: Harper and Row, 1964.

"Singles Lifestyle Gains Acceptance, Pollsters Report," *Arizona Republic*, April 1983.

Sommer, Robert. *Tight Spaces: Hard Architecture and How to Humanize It*. Englewood Cliffs, N.J.: Prentice-Hall, Inc., 1974.

Spiegel, John, and P. Mackotka. *Messages of the Body*. New York: The Free Press, 1974.

Stoller, L. "The Masculine Mystique," *Givavdanian*, 1975.

Tannahill, Reay. *Sex in History*. New York: Stein and Day, 1980.

Toffler, Alvin. *The Third Wave*. New York: Bantam Books, 1980.

Wolf, Linda. *The Cosmo Report*. New York: Arbor House, 1981.

Worringer, Wilhelm. *Form in Gothic*. New York: Schocken Books, 1967.

"Words of Love—Old Valentines Reflect a Change of Heart," *Arizona Republic*, 1983.

Wright, Lawrence. *Warm and Snug: The History of the Bed*. London: Routledge and Kegan Paul, 1962.

Yankelovich, Daniel. *New Rules: Searching for Self-Fulfillment in a World Turned Upside Down*. New York: Random House, 1981.

Zaslow, Jeffrey. "Aroma di Amore," *Orlando Sentinel*, July 1982.

List of Designers

Dennis Abbé
246 West End Ave.
New York, NY 10023

Eric Bernard Designs
177 East 94th St.
New York, NY 10020

James Blakely III, ASID
P.O. Box 5173
Beverly Hills, CA 90210

Agnes Bourne
1955 Mountain Blvd.
Oakland, CA 94611

Bray & Schaible
Robert Bray
Michael Schaible
80 West 40th St.
New York, NY 10018

Doris Bruno Design Studio
1172 Brickyard Rd.
Salt Lake City, UT 84106

Charles Burke International
329 West Wetherly Dr.
Suite 207
Beverly Hills, CA 90210

James Callahan
1074 North Palm Canyon
Palm Springs, CA 92262

Steven Chase Associates
69846 Highway 111
Rancho Mirage, CA 92270

Michael Coffey, Artist
Gallery 10
New York, NY

Joyce Colton, ASID, FISID
Ron Hines, ISID
P.O. Box 8171
Van Nuys, CA 91401

Barbara D'Arcy, ASID
Bloomingdale's
1000 Third Ave.
New York, NY 10022

Barbara Dorn Associates, Inc.
Joszi Meskin, Designer
2417 Franklin St.
San Francisco, CA 94123

Ron Fields, ASID
10509 Wilkins
Los Angeles, CA 90024

Charlotte Finn
New York, NY

Ellen Finn, Artist
Box 3572
Art Department
New Mexico State University
Las Cruces, NM 88001

Billy Gaylord & Associates
1555 Pacific Ave.
San Francisco, CA 94019

Arnold Goldstein, Artist
55 West 26th St.
New York, NY 10010

Douglas Pierce Hiatt, AISD, ISID, CPID
Hiatt Enterprises International, Inc.
9701 Wilshire Blvd.
Suite 710
Beverly Hills, CA 90212

Insights, Inc.
Brice Goers
1997 Lake Ave.
Highland Park, IL 60035

David James Design
8262 Fountain Circle
Los Angeles, CA 90046

Leza Lidow
P.O. Box 446
El Segundo, CA 90245

Sam Lopata, Architect
New York, NY

David S. Miller, AIBD
1400 Yosemite Ave.
San Francisco, CA 94124

Bob Mitchell, ASID
3211 South La Cienega Blvd.
Los Angeles, CA 90016

Phyllis Morris Showrooms
8772 Beverly Blvd.
Los Angeles, CA 90048

Olivia Neece, ASID, IBD
18200 Rosita St.
Tarzana, CA 91356

Richard Ohrbach, ASID
Lynn Jacobson, ASID
941 Park Ave.
New York, NY 10020

Paul Rudolph, Architect
54 West 57th St.
New York, NY 10019

Graham Smith and Associates
145 East 35th St.
New York, NY 10016

Versailles Collection
Suzanne Dahl
Jerry Barich
8687 Melrose Ave.
Los Angeles, CA 90069

David Winfield Wilson
San Francisco, CA

List of Manufacturers

Many of the manufacturers and showrooms listed below can only be contacted through your local interior designers or the designers listed on the preceding page.

Allmilmo
P.O. Box 629 A6
Fairfield, NJ 10700

Artebella, Incorporated
8687 Melrose Ave.
Los Angeles, CA 90069

Artistic Brass
4100 Ardmore Ave.
Los Angeles, CA 92080

Avento
200 Lexington Ave.
New York, NY 10016

Bob Mitchell Designs
Culver City, CA

Bolae Collection
4874 Southwest 75th St.
Miami, FL 33155

Brass Bottom, Inc.
177 F. Riverside Ave.
Newport Beach, CA 92663

Brueton Industries, Inc.
227-02 145th St.
Springfield Gardens, NY 11413

Brunschwig and Fils, Inc.
410 East 62nd St.
New York, NY 10021

Brueton Industries
979 Third Ave.
New York, NY 10022

Casa Nova
979 Third Ave.
New York, NY 10022

Casella Lighting
111 Rhode Island St.
San Francisco, CA 94103

Celler Masters, Inc.
2029 Century Park E.
Los Angeles, CA 90067

Cowtan and Tout
979 Third Ave.
New York, NY 10022

Devin, Inc.
4801 Exposition Blvd.
Los Angeles, CA 90016

Donghia Furniture
306 East 61st St.
New York, NY 10021

Edward Pashayan and Co.
305 East 63rd St.
New York, NY 10021

Elodia, Inc.
240 bb Thunderbird Drive
El Paso, TX 79912

Farallon Studio
Spring Street
Sausalito, CA 94965

Fran Murphy, Inc.
401 Clematis St.
Palm Beach, FL 33480

Gia International Design
430 59th St.
New York, NY 10022

Guerlain, Inc.
444 Madison Ave.
New York, NY 10022

Hastings Tile Co.
964 Third Ave.
New York, NY 10022

Innovational Marketing
P.O. Box 26386
San Diego, CA 92126

International Down Shops
2915 Red Hill #G-102
Costa Mesa, CA 92627

IPF International, Inc.
11-13 Maryland Ave.
Paterson, NJ 07503

Jacuzzi
P.O. Drawer J
Walnut Creek, CA 94596

Karl Mann and Associates
232 East 59th St.
New York, NY 10022

Katzenbach and Warren, Inc.
950 Third Ave.
New York, NY 10022

Kohler Company
Kohler, WI 53044

La Maison Edery, Inc.
477 Madison Ave.
New York, NY 10022

Lightolier
346 Claremont Ave.
Jersey City, NJ 07405

La Verne Galleries
3925 N. Miami Ave.
Miami, FL 33137

Lighting Associates, Inc.
305 East 63rd St.
New York, NY 10021

Marc II Gallery
8747 Melrose Ave.
Los Angeles, CA 90069

Martin Klein Design
11661 San Vincente Blvd.
Los Angeles, CA 90049

Merit Carpet Corp.
3410 Century Circle
Irvine, TX 75062

Myson
P.O. Box 5025
Falmouth, VA 22403

Neoray
537 Johnson Ave.
Brooklyn, NY 11237

Norman of Salisbury
P.O. Box 799
Salisbury, NC 28144

Oggetti
48 Northwest 25th St.
Miami, FL 33127

Rahmanan
440 Park Ave.
New York, NY 10016

Roland Kenfield
1104 Lincoln Ave.
San Rafael, CA 94901

Rollamatic Roofs, Inc.
1400 Yosemite Ave.
San Francisco, CA 94124

Rosecore
979 Third Ave.
New York, NY 10022

Sherle Wagner International
165 East 72nd St.
New York, NY 10021

S. Harris and Co., Inc.
580 S. Douglas St.
El Segundo, CA 90245

Stendig Inc.
410 62nd St.
New York, NY 10021

Swaim Originals
P.O. Box 4147
High Point, NC 21263

Paul Associates
155 East 55th St.
New York, NY 10022

Paul Evans Studio
306 East 61st St.
New York, NY 10021

Teakwood, Inc.
P.O. Box 47339
Atlanta, GA 30362

Terri Roese Silks, Inc.
413 North Oak St.
Inglewood, CA 90302

Thayer Coggins, Inc.
467 South Rd.
High Point, NC 27262

The Brass Bed
4238 N. Scottsdale Rd.
Scottsdale, AZ 85251

The Wicker Works
650 Potrero Ave.
San Francisco, CA 94110

Versailles Collection, Inc.
Pacific Design Center
8687 Melrose Ave.
Los Angeles, CA 90069

Youngjohann Hillman, Inc.
1350 Manufacturing
Suite 188
Dallas, TX 75207

Index

Italics indicate illustrations.